Ten Pearls of Wisdom

of Wisdom

from Ecclesiastes

by Woodrow Kroll

BACK TO THE BIBLE
Publishing

TEN PEARLS OF WISDOM
published by Back to the Bible
©1998 by Woodrow Kroll

International Standard Book Number
0-8474-0695-4

Edited by Rachel Derowitsch
Cover concept by Laura Goodspeed

For information:
BACK TO THE BIBLE
POST OFFICE BOX 82808
LINCOLN, NEBRASKA 68501
1 2 3 4 5 6 7 8 9—04 03 02 01 00 99 98

Printed in the USA

CONTENTS

If you've ever had anyone give you some nuggets of their wisdom, you know how disappointing it can be when you find out they were wrong. If someone gives you a stock tip or suggests who the starting quarterback for your favorite team will be, you may value their insight and act accordingly. But if that insight proves to be faulty, their "wisdom" will only cause you grief.

The pearls of wisdom you gain from God's Word, however, are not at all like man's. The greatest repository of wisdom in the world is found in the Bible. Most Christians would agree with that, and they would assume that I'm talking about God's wisdom—the knowledge of the all-knowing God. But that's not the case. Of course, God's wisdom is the greatest wisdom possible; but in the Bible you'll find not only the great wisdom of God, but the greatest wisdom of man as well.

In the Book of Ecclesiastes, you'll discover the wisdom of the wisest man who ever lived, Solomon. Although this relatively brief book of the Bible is full of pearls of wisdom, we will consider only ten of the most brilliant ones. These pearls talk about life and money, about unity and time and many other important topics. It's not only smart wisdom—practical and useful—but most important, it's also inspired of God, and that's an unbeatable combination.

Show me someone who is schooled in the wisdom of the Bible, and I'll show you a truly wise man or woman. Once you have learned the pearls of God's Word, you will have gained immeasurable wisdom, both for living in this world and for preparing for the next.

CHAPTER ONE

God's Time

Pearl of Wisdom
"To everything there is a season, a time for
every purpose under heaven."
Ecclesiastes 3:1

Our lives revolve around time. If I asked you what time it is, I have a pretty good idea what you'd do. You'd glance at your watch, check the time and respond appropriately. If you were enjoying what you were doing at the moment, you might exclaim, "My, how time flies!" If you weren't especially happy about what you were doing, you'd probably groan, "Is it only _____?" Time has been the theme of ballads like "As Time Goes By," and a common excuse for many failures is, "I didn't have time." Most of us check our watch several times a day—or several times an hour. Sometimes we do it more often than we should, like when we're in church. All of this only goes to show how involved we are with time.

But actually, time, as we know it, is a very recent phenomenon. Through the persistence of Charles Dodd, a schoolteacher, and William Allen, a railroad engineer, time was finally standardized in the United States on November 10, 1883. It was only after American railroads accepted Dodd and Allen's idea of four time zones across the United States that trains could schedule their arrivals and departures with any degree of consistency. Before that, every community decided what time it was on their own. It took another year for a meeting of 26 nations to determine the 24-hour worldwide time zones that we use today.

Nor have we always had seven days in our week. Back in 1792 the French tried a ten-day week with ten hours in a day, 100 minutes in an hour and 100 seconds in a minute. But it didn't work. Undaunted, the Russians tried a five-day week in 1929 and even named the days of the week after colors. But nobody paid any attention, so the Russians switched to a six-day week in 1932. Finally they abandoned the whole idea and returned to the standard seven-day week.

Although the way we describe time hasn't been around all that long, God has been working with time since the beginning of creation. In fact, He's the originator of time. The first mention of time is in Genesis 1:5: "So the evening and the morning were the first day." But the great time chapter of the Bible is Ecclesiastes 3. In this chapter the word *time* occurs on 28 occasions in 14 pairs of polar opposites divided into seven groups. Seven, the number of completeness, suggests that these contrasting pairs cover almost every conceivable experience of man, beginning with birth and ending with death.

So what time is it for you? How are you using your time? What does time hold in store for you? Perhaps you will find answers to some of your time questions in the time chapter, Ecclesiastes 3.

Season and time

The first phrase in Ecclesiastes 3:1 gives us the right perspective on time: "To everything there is a season, and a time for every purpose under heaven." The two words here—*season* and *time*—imply duration and a point in time. Because everything has a season, nothing (at least on earth) lasts forever. God has appointed a "season" for everything. Seasons have beginnings and endings. They last, but not too long. In the life cycle there is a season for gestation, a season for childhood and youth, a season for middle age and a season for old age, followed by death. It's all quite natural; it's all ordained by God.

The word translated "time" means "a point in time." Within any give season, there is a point in time in which God has ordained everything to happen. Within the season of our older youth, my wife and I decided to get married. We were in the season of our 20s, but the time was June 26. So *season* means a period of time and *time* means a point in time.

Solomon's thesis is this: Every activity of mankind has a proper time and a predetermined duration. Our lives will be a lot less stressful if we recognize that the omniscient hand of God has appointed a time when things are to be done, and He has a predetermined duration for those things to last.

Examples of polar opposites

Solomon now demonstrates how this process of time fitting into a season takes place. For example, verse 2 says, "A time to be born, and a time to die; a time to plant, and a time to pluck what is planted." Nature has a season of growth, but within that season there is a time to plant and a time to harvest. Sowing first, then, after a duration, harvesting. How often we allow the tyranny of time to rob us of the patience of seasons.

There's also the process of constructing and destroying, or tearing down. A building is built in a few months, and then, 50 years or so later, that building is torn down. The destruction of the building is usually faster than its construction, but the duration (season) is always longer than either the time of building or the time of tearing down.

Verse 5 says, "A time to cast away stones, and a time to gather stones." Again, using the image of building, Solomon says, "There's a time to cast away the stones from your fields so that you can farm the field. And then there's a time to pick up those stones on the edge of the field and build a house with them." Building and rebuilding are what the seasons of our lives are all about.

Verse 6 continues this thought: "A time to gain, and a time to lose; a time to keep, and a time to throw away." There is a time to go shopping (the time your wife likes best) and a time to throw old, useless things away (the time she hates the most). If you're a shopper by nature—you have that extra shopping gene that impels you to drop everything and go shopping—you know how easy it is to enjoy the time for acquiring new things. But do you have the same disposition when it comes time to part with those things? After the season of usefulness, the time to gain is past; the time to throw away has come. I have to admit, the pain of this time has been greatly reduced with the invention of the garage sale. There is duration—a season of time—for everything, and then there is a point in time for change.

Solomon's example of polar opposites in verse 7 may seem strange to you: "A time to tear, and a time to sew." In the Middle East, tearing was a sign of mourning. Sewing your clothes after the mourning period was over was the signal to return to a life of joy. Remember when Job's three friends came to comfort him? The first thing Eliphaz, Bildad and Zophar did was weep. Then "each one tore his robe and sprinkled dust on his head toward heaven" (Job 2:12). There is a time to show that you're commiserating with someone—a time to tear your gown. But then there's also a time to move beyond your sorrow and to sew the gown again.

Everyone goes through good times and bad times; together they make up the season of your life. It's not the times of our lives that shape us, but the seasons. Make sure you don't live only for the good times; when the bad times come, and they will, you won't have the strength to handle them. And make sure you don't let the bad times defeat you. If you do, you'll miss out on all the good times God still has in store for you. It takes both to make a life. Make certain your attitude toward life is such that, even if you can't enjoy all the times, you do enjoy the season. Praise God that neither good times nor bad times last; only eternity does.

Even the polar opposites in verse 8 can be understood if we place time into the arena of duration: "A time to love, and a time to hate; a time of war, and a time of peace." Of course, Solomon is not advocating either hate or war. But the reality is, there are things for us to hate (the things God hates), and there may be a time for us to fight (as God's people, Israel, did). His point is that we are to balance all the times of our lives so that the season pleases God. That's a pearl of wisdom. If things aren't going your way, give it time. If things are going your way, prepare for the time when they won't. Set your sights on the duration season, not on the peaks and valleys of time. Build your life on God's Word and you will be a seasoned Christian. Build your life on the things that happen in time, and you will be a soured Christian.

All things beautiful

Why does Solomon say all these things about time? The answer is found in verse 11: "He [God] has made everything beautiful in its time." At the appropriate point in time, God will make everything fit into the season of your life. It's like the pieces of a puzzle. You struggle to piece things together, and then all of a sudden things just seem to fall into place. That's what happens when you commit both your times and your seasons to God.

The word translated "beautiful" doesn't mean "lovely" or "pretty." It means "fitting," "appropriate" or "proper." There is a fitting point in time that God has determined something should happen. Accordingly, God will never be late and He'll never be early. Furthermore, He knows the proper duration for that event. He never holds it over too long or cuts it off too short.

In the same fashion, God knows the most fitting points and the most appropriate seasons of our lives as well. He knows exactly the number of days He's given to you, and nobody can shorten those days; nobody can lengthen them either. Our times and seasons are in God's hand. And what we entrust to God's hand, God makes "proper" in its time.

So what does that mean—God makes everything fitting or proper in its own time? Consider the polar opposites in verse 2 again as an example: "A time to be born, and a time to die." Is it possible that God can make even death beautiful in its time? He can. At the proper time, God makes death fitting. He makes it appropriate. He makes it proper. There is a time for us to be born—a day in which God determines we will be born—and there's also a day in which God determines that our life on this side of the grave will end. A time to be born, and a time to die. To shorten our days through suicide or to lengthen them through heroic care fails to demonstrate faith in God's ability to know the proper season of our lives.

After Jacob had seen his long-lost son Joseph, he said, "Now let me die, since I have seen your face, because you are still alive" (Gen. 46:30). He knew his days had been fulfilled. The duration—the season—was done. The exact day of his death was in God's hands. But Jacob knew this season of his life had reached its completion.

Going according to plan

If God has already determined the times and seasons of our lives, is it possible to die before our time? In a sense it is. Solomon exhorted, "Do not be overly wicked, nor be foolish: why should you die before your time?" (Eccles. 7:17). Through wickedness or self-will, we can deprive ourselves of the fullness of days that God would have liked to have given us, but even this must be approved by God and is a part of His eternal plan.

For a believer, the thought that not only do we have a time to be born, but there is a set duration before our death, is a tremendous comfort. It means everything is going according to God's plan. The apostle John said, "Then I heard a voice from heaven saying to me, 'Write: 'Blessed are the dead who die in the Lord'" (Rev. 14:13). The psalmist added, "Precious in the sight of the LORD is the death of his saints" (Ps. 116:15). Of course, we still don't look forward to death. And when death comes to our family—to our spouse, to our little children, to our parents—we always say, "Why, Lord? Why now?" But we must never forget that God has a duration for our life. In God's grace He will not allow one day more or one day less than that duration. It's all according to His divine plan.

And here's one final and exciting possibility within God's plan. It is also possible that those in Christ will never die. In 1 Thessalonians 4:17, Paul says, "Then we who are alive and remain shall be caught up together with them in the clouds to meet the Lord in the air. And thus we shall always be with the Lord." It is possible that the season of our lives will simply be swallowed up in the eternity of God. The omnipotent One can interrupt the sequence of "a time to be born and a time to die," and one day He will do just that. Perhaps today!

Whether God chooses to take us to Himself through the blessing of death or the blessed hope, in God's plan we end up being with Him forever. Instead of fretting about the days of our lives or worrying about how long we will live, life would be more enjoyable if we simply rested in the Lord and committed all those days to Him, including our final days.

In a world of heroic medical care and wonder drugs, let's not forget that just as the day of our birth was part of God's eternal timetable, so is the day of our death. None of us likes the idea of facing death, but those who have trusted Jesus Christ as Savior can face it very differently than those who are fearing the consequences of their sin. For believers, the day of our death is another day to glorify the Lord. The day when we die is simply another day to commit to a loving and omniscient God. The day of our death is, in His hands, every bit as wonderful as the day of our birth. "This is the day which the Lord has made; we will rejoice and be glad in it" (Ps. 118:24).

When you live and die in the knowledge of God's eternal plan, you live and die with this confidence—God makes all things beautiful in their time.

Are you tired of everything in your life going wrong? Are you fed up with trying to make things in your life lovely and easy and pleasant, only to have them turn out messy and hard and distasteful? Maybe you've gone the whole route. You've been through alcohol, you've been through drugs, you've been through sex addiction, you've been through climbing the ladder of success—and your life is still a colossal mess. But don't give up yet. There is an answer. The answer is Jesus Christ in your life. It's through faith in Jesus Christ as your Savior that God can make your life beautiful, and He does it in His own time. And maybe—just maybe—this is God's time for you. Let Him make your life beautiful.

CHAPTER TWO

Procastination

Pearl of Wisdom
"Whatever your hand finds to do, do it
with your might; for there is no work
or device or knowledge or wisdom in the
grave where you are going."
Ecclesiastes 9:10

Are you familiar with Elisha Gray? Probably not. But I'm sure you've heard of Alexander Graham Bell, the man who invented the telephone. Well, Elisha Gray was a Chicago electrician. He filed a patent application for the telephone two hours after Alexander Graham Bell did. A small delay of only two hours cost Elisha Gray fame and an enormous fortune.

It's little wonder that Ecclesiastes counsels us not to procrastinate: "Whatever your hand finds to do, do it with your might." Urgency is reflected in this pearl of wisdom because, as so many have already discovered, tomorrow is never guaranteed.

Ancient mythology depicts time as being like a man who has long hair in front but is bald in back. The point is that you must catch hold of time coming toward you because after it's past, nothing is left to grab.

When God calls us to a particular task, we need to respond by doing it now and doing it well. Throw everything into whatever God gives you to do. Take whatever

God has put in your hand and use it without delay and without reserve for the Lord.

In Genesis 22, Abraham and Isaac went to the top of Mount Moriah. God put into Abraham's hand two things: a son and a knife. And Abraham was willing to use the knife on his only son to please God. In David's hand God put two things. He put a small sling and a small bag holding five smooth stones. It wasn't very much against the giant Goliath, but it was all David needed because God was on his side. Whatever God placed into David's hand, David used mightily (1 Sam. 17:40-50). Into Moses' hand God placed only one thing, a rod. When God asked Moses what was in his hand, he said, "It's just a rod." But when Moses cast it down according to God's instructions, it became a serpent and the symbol of God's authority in Moses' life (Ex. 4).

That's always been God's question to His people and it's His question to you today: "What do you have in your hand?" Whatever you have in your hand today—a saucepan, a computer, the wheel of an automobile, a Bible—that's what God is looking for you to use. He's looking for you to use it now and with all your might.

It's legitimate for us to ask why. Why should we do it with all our might? Let me suggest several reasons to you from God's Word.

Because we are imitators of Christ

The Bible says that all who are saved are to be like our Savior. Isaiah 50:7 prophetically records the words of the Messiah: "For the LORD God will help Me; therefore I will not be disgraced; therefore I have set My face like a flint, and I know that I will not be ashamed." If Jesus could set His face like a flint to do what God gave Him to do (Luke 9:51), shouldn't we do the same? Hebrews 12:1-2 tells us, "Therefore we also, since we are surrounded by so great a cloud of witnesses, let us lay aside every weight, and the sin which so easily ensnares us [or besets us], and let us run with endurance the race that is set before us, looking unto Jesus, the author and finisher of our faith"—now notice this—"who for the joy that was set before Him endured the cross, despising the shame, and has sat down at the right hand of the throne of God." Jesus did well what God had for Him to do. He did it with intensity. He set His face like a flint. He even looked past the shame and the suffering to the joy of doing the will of the Father.

If you and I are to imitate Christ, we have to adapt His attitude of fervency. Whatever God puts into our hands to do, we need to do it as if it were the last opportunity we'll ever have to do it. It may well be. Whatever God gives you to do, do it with all your might because your Savior did and you want to be just like Him.

Because God created us with potential

You have the potential of doing great things for your Master. God created every human with enormous capacity, but unless you serve the Lord with fervency, you'll never reach that capacity. The apostle Paul reminds us that Jesus Himself "gave some to be apostles, some prophets, some evangelists,

19

and some pastors and teachers, for the equipping of the saints for the work of the ministry, for the edifying of the body of Christ, till we all come to the unity of the faith and the knowledge of the Son of God, to be a perfect [complete] man, to the measure of the stature of the fullness of Christ; that we should no longer be children, tossed to and fro and carried about with every wind of doctrine, . . . but . . . may grow up in all things into Him who is the Head—Christ" (Eph. 4:11-15). What those verses tell us is simply this: Jesus Christ is our full potential. You and I need to become like Him in all things. When we are able to reflect His character in every dimension of our lives—His love, purity, honesty, etc.— then we've reached our full potential in Him. Unfortunately, that full potential remains a distant dream for so many Christians.

When you first came to trust Jesus as Savior, you were just a babe in Christ. You were just "getting into" this faith thing. You were just beginning to understand what heaven is all about. But if you've been a Christian for a year, 10 years, 40 years, you're not at the "getting in" place any more. You should be moving on, well on your way to growing up in Christ.

It's like the little boy who kept falling out of bed. His mother would carry him to his room and kiss him good night. But morning after morning she would find him sleeping on the floor alongside his bed. She wondered why until she noticed that the little guy never crawled completely into bed at night. Instead, he would throw one leg over the side of the bed and let the other dangle toward the floor. As soon as he rolled over, plop, he would fall on the floor. When his mother described the problem to him, the little boy correctly observed, "I guess I stay too close to the getting in place."

That's so true with a great number of Christians. When they're saved, they stay too close to the "getting in place." They remain spiritual babies all their lives. They feed on little Bible treats instead of enjoying a solid diet of the deep things of God's Word. They prefer spiritual junk food to a hearty meal. They are addicted to the spiritual equivalent of Gummi Bears when they should be building strong spiritual bones by eating God's green beans.

That doesn't have to be the case, of course. What we need is to get back to the Bible and spend sufficient time in it to understand the deeper things of God's Word. And when we do, we find out that God created us with a potential that's far beyond where we are right now.

Because the time is limited

Why should we do everything we do for God with all our might? Why should we seize every available opportunity to be used of Him? Because the opportunity for service to God is only for a very limited time.

A day comes for every person when death shuts the door on all opportunities for service to the Lord. In Psalm 6:5 David laments, "For in death there is no remembrance of You; in the grave who will give You thanks?" And Paul urges, "Let us walk properly, as in the day, not in revelry or drunkenness, not in licentiousness and lewdness, not in strife and envy" (Rom. 13:13). Today, right now, is the day we need to do what God gives us to do because we don't know how many days we have left.

J. Allen Petersen wrote about a trip he and his wife took to the beach. As he was lying there he looked at his wife and said, "You know, honey, I'm 56. I'm middle-aged!" She replied, "How many men do you know who live to be over 112?"

How old are you today? Are you middle-aged or beyond? How long do you expect to live? And what do you know about tomorrow? What guarantees do you have that you'll have another 50 years or even 10 years to serve the Lord? You don't have those guarantees. That's why it's important that "whatever your hand finds to do, do it with your might; for there is no work or device or knowledge or wisdom in the grave where you're going."

Here's that same pearl of wisdom said another way by Jesus, "I must work the works of Him who sent Me while it is day; the night is coming when no one can work" (John 9:4). We have all eternity to enjoy the fruit of our labors here on earth, but we have only a few short hours before the sunset in which to work. We can't afford to wait. Whatever God calls and gifts us to do, we have to do it now and with all our might.

A personal response

Every morning when I get up I ask the Lord to help me do several things. First, I ask Him to help me live purely during the day, with clean hands and a pure heart. I don't think anything else I do is important if I'm not pure before God. Second, I ask Him to help me see everything I have to do today with an eternal perspective.

Many things clamor for my attention. There are lots of topics I could address on our daily *Back to the Bible* broadcast that would help you in time, but would they change you for eternity? Frankly, I'm not interested in those things that are for this time only. I know I have only a few short hours before sunset to do what God will enable me to do that's important for all eternity. That's why this pearl of wisdom is so important to me. Whatever my hand finds to do, I must do it well and I must do it now. Yesterday is like a canceled check. Tomorrow is a promissory note. Today is like ready cash. We must use this day wisely, for today is the most precious possession that we have.

"Whatever your hand finds to do, do it with all your might." Don't procrastinate in serving the Lord and don't ever serve Him in a wimpy manner. Halfhearted service is not only not hearty, it's only barely alive. When you do for the Lord what He asks you to do in a halfhearted way, you're not living up to your potential in Christ.

So what is God asking you to do today? Is it helping make crafts for a Sunday school lesson? Is it teaching a Bible class or preparing a devotional for a family gathering? Is it supporting a missionary on the field? Is it praying for your pastor and your church? Is it telling your neighbor about the Lord Jesus? What does He want from you right now? No one can answer that question but you, and you must. Likely you already know what God wants you to do. The only question is, will you do it halfheartedly or wholeheartedly? Will you throw yourself into it? Will you give it the very best that you have? Will you do for God all that God wants you to do?

"Whatever your hand finds to do, do it with your might; for there is no work or device or knowledge or wisdom in the grave where you're going." That's one of God's priceless pearls of wisdom. Whatever God is impressing upon you to do today, do it now. Do it with all your might. Who knows? You may have only today in which to do it.

Church historians tell us that the 18th-century saint Count Nikolaus Von Zinzendorf, founder of the Moravian Church, owed much of his religious zeal to the viewing of a picture of the crucifixion. Underneath was the inscription, "All this for thee; how much for Me!" Never again could he tarry in serving the Lord. Never again could he make just a halfhearted effort.

How about you?

CHAPTER THREE

Silver Doesn't Satisfy

Pearl of Wisdom
"He who loves silver will not be satisfied
with silver; nor he who loves abundance
with increase. This also is vanity."
Ecclesiastes 5:10

There is a popular commercial today that features kids, sports announcers, celebrities and ordinary men and women all singing the jingle "If I could be like Mike." They're singing, of course, about basketball superstar Michael Jordan.

Arguably the best player the game has ever seen, Michael Jordan makes more than $300,000 dollars a game. That's about $10,000 a minute, assuming he plays 30 minutes per game. That's likely more than you make in a year—and for some people, in a lifetime! But that's not all. Jordan is the king of endorsements for all kinds of products ranging from breakfast cereal to underwear. Assuming that Michael earns another $40 million in endorsements during the year, he makes $178,100 a day, whether he works or not. What's more, assuming that he sleeps seven hours a night, that means he makes $52,000 every night—while he's sleeping! If Michael Jordan goes to see a movie, it will cost him approximately $7; but during that time he'll make $18,550. If he decides to have a three-minute egg, while that egg is boiling he will make $370. Let's suppose that Michael decided to save up for a new car—say, an Acura NSX. Do you know how long it would take him to save for this $90,000 car? All of 12 hours.

If you were given a tenth of a penny for every dollar that Michael makes, you'd be living comfortably at $65,000 a year. And think about this. In 1998 Michael Jordan made more than twice as much as all of our U.S. presidents for all of their terms of office combined. I know that sounds incredible, but it's true. And if you can take one more mind-numbing comparison, consider this: Michael Jordan would have to save 100 percent of his income for 270 years just to have the same net worth as Bill Gates of Microsoft!

Now I don't want to put a pin in this bubble of success, but the Bible has some very sobering things to say about money, and one of them is found in Ecclesiastes 5:10. This pearl of wisdom says, "He who loves silver will not be satisfied with silver; nor he who loves abundance with increase. This also is vanity." You can always use more, but no matter how much more you get, you will not be satisfied.

You're probably familiar with the expression "Money isn't everything, but it's way ahead of whatever is in second place." We all feel like that sometimes, but do you know that there are lots of things money cannot do? The Bible highlights several things money cannot do for you.

Money cannot satisfy a hungry soul

Ben Franklin, the great American statesmen, said, "Money never made a man happy yet, nor will it. There is nothing in its nature to produce happiness. The more a man has, the more he wants. Instead of it filling a vacuum, it makes one. If it satisfies one want, it doubles and triples that want another way." Franklin was right. One of the things money cannot do is satisfy the hungry soul.

You may be making a wonderful salary. You're sitting pretty where you are, you've climbed the ladder of success, you've put some away in the bank, you have a nicely balanced investment portfolio—yet you may be spiritually hungry. You cry out to God because you are empty. Nothing in your assets can give you joy. Your broker may be satisfied but your soul isn't.

There's just more to life than money. One of the facts about corporate life is that the average chief executive of a company today works 60 hours-plus every week of his life. And yet, at an unprecedented rate, CEOs of large corporations making enormous salaries are leaving their companies because they can't handle the emptiness. Solomon said, "Again, I saw that for all toil and every skillful work a man is envied by his neighbor. This also is vanity and grasping for the wind. The fool folds his hands and consumes his own flesh. Better is a handful with quietness than both hands full, together with toil and grasping for the wind. Then I returned, and I saw vanity under the sun" (Eccles. 4:4-7).

Now ponder what the wealthy king of Israel said next: "There is one alone, without companion: he has neither son nor brother.

Yet there is no end to all his labors, nor is his eye satisfied with riches" (v. 8).

Regardless of your situation in life, you can never satisfy a hungry soul with money. There is a big God-shaped hole in the middle of your heart that can be satisfied only by God. Try as you may, money will never satisfy your hungry soul. Only God can do that.

Money can't enrich a greedy soul

In Acts 8, an evangelist by the name of Philip was preaching in the city of Samaria. While there, many people trusted Jesus Christ as Savior. People were healed of infirmities and diseases, and other good things happened while he was ministering in this city. Among those who made professions of faith was a sorcerer named Simon. He was not only saved but also baptized. However, "when Simon saw that through laying on of the apostles' hands the Holy Spirit was given, he offered them money, saying, 'Give me this power also, that anyone on whom I lay hands may receive the Holy Spirit.' But Peter said to him, 'Your money will perish with you, because you thought that the gift of God could be purchased with money!'" (Acts 8:18). A greedy man like Simon will always walk away disappointed because God's gifts can't be bought.

Money cannot buy everything. And it's not that people haven't tried. With the advent of plastic money, the credit card has been used to run up the largest consumer debt in history. People have literally attempted to buy happiness. But these same people, now saddled with the weight of enormous debt, are miserable.

Consistently over the years surveys have shown that regardless of how much money we have, and regardless of our standard of living, the average person considers that about 20 percent more money would make him happy. That's all we need—just a little more. It doesn't matter how much we already have; if only we had 20 percent more we'd really be happy. But money cannot enrich a greedy soul.

Howard Hughes was one of the richest men in the world, and yet from what we know he lived a joyless, half-lunatic life. In his later years, Hughes fled from one resort hotel to another—from Las Vegas to Nicaragua to Acapulco. His physical appearance became progressively odder as he grew older. At the end, his straggly beard hung down to his waist. He had hair that reached down to the middle of his back. His fingernails were two inches long. He had toenails that hadn't been trimmed in so long they resembled corkscrews.

Early in his life, Howard Hughes married Jean Peters, a movie star, one of the most beautiful women in the world. They were married for 13 years. But in that 13-year period, no one ever saw them together in public. There is no record of his ever having been photographed with his wife. Hughes once said, "Every man has his price, or a guy like me couldn't exist." And yet when he died, most of his employees who have broken their silence reported their disgust for him. Money couldn't satisfy his greedy soul.

Money can't redeem a doomed soul

In Zephaniah 1:14-15 we read, "The great day of the LORD is near; it is near and hastens quickly. The noise of the day of the LORD is bitter; there the mighty men shall cry out. That day is a day of wrath, a day of trouble and distress, a day of devastation and desolation, a day of darkness and gloominess, a day of clouds and thick darkness, a day of trumpet and alarm against the fortified cities and against the high towers.'"

Zephaniah is talking about the day of God's judgment. He continues in verses 17-18: "I will bring distress upon men, and they shall walk like blind men, because they have sinned against the LORD; their blood shall be poured out like dust, and their flesh like refuse. Neither their silver nor their gold shall be able to deliver them in the day of the Lord's wrath."

The day of God's judgment will come. That's one of the certainties of life. But what are you going to do on the day that God will judge you? Will you whip out your checkbook and try to buy your way out of God's wrath? Will you cash in some of your CDs and say, "Look, God, this is what I have. It's all Yours. Just deliver me from the doom of my own soul"? No one can buy his way out of destruction. Money can't deliver anyone from the consequences of their sin.

And what's more, money cannot deliver a nation from the wrath of God. If money couldn't deliver Solomon's Israel from her sin, if money couldn't deliver Caesar's Rome from her sin, I wonder what makes Americans think that money can deliver America from her sin? If you're not an American,

30

what about your country? Are your national leaders assuming that somehow they can buy their way out of national sin, collective sin or personal sin? In the day when God's great wrath falls in judgment (Rev. 6:17), money will be of no use to anyone.

Someone has suggested that the real measure of our wealth is how much we'd be worth if we lost all of our money. So how much are you worth? No one begrudges anyone else the money they have made honestly, whether by investing or working hard or through a family inheritance. Indeed, the Bible says that when we have that kind of wealth, we have a gift from God (Eccles. 5:18-19). God doesn't say it is wrong to be rich. What God's Word says is we can't rely on our riches (Job 31:24-28).

Read the call of Isaiah, the prophet. He says, "Ho! Everyone who thirsts, come to the waters; and you who have no money, come, buy and eat. Yes, come, buy wine and milk without money and without price" (Isa. 55:1-2). Those verses tell us that salvation, the redemption of our lost souls, has nothing to do with money. Peter says, "Knowing that you were not redeemed with corruptible things, like silver or gold, . . . but with the precious blood of Christ, as of a lamb without blemish and without spot" (1 Pet. 1:18-19). Do you know what purchased your redemption? It was the obedience of Jesus Christ at the cross of Calvary. He died to pay the penalty for your sin. That which can redeem your lost soul is not your checkbook, not your numbered bank account, not your CDs, not your retirement fund, but the blood of Jesus Christ.

What can you trust?

Do yourself a favor. Take some time and think about all the blessings you have from the hand of God. Think about the things that didn't cost you any money at all. In fact, why not make a list of them and share them with your friends as a testimony to the Lord? It's good for us to see once in a while just how very little money can do for us in an eternal way. Certainly we need money to live. We need it in daily commerce. None of us ever seems to have enough. It takes money to continue a ministry like this one at Back to the Bible. It takes money to clothe and feed your family. It takes money to purchase a home. But there are so many people who think it takes money to live, and it doesn't. Real life—eternal life, saving life—is the free gift of God.

Have you trusted Jesus Christ today to be your Savior, or are you still trusting your money? Money cannot satisfy a hungry soul. Money cannot enrich a greedy soul. Money cannot deliver a doomed soul. And money cannot redeem a lost soul. If you're looking for eternal redemption, if you're looking for a future in heaven, you need to trust the blood of Jesus Christ. Trust Him as your Savior. That's the way to get God's redemption.

Here's a real pearl of wisdom. All the money in the world cannot do for you what one act of obedience at Calvary's cross did for you. You can hoard money. You can amass great wealth. You can build a sound financial portfolio. But one day you will leave it all behind. In fact, most people don't fully enjoy it while they have it. But that

which is not bought with silver or gold—
your eternal redemption in Christ Jesus—
can be enjoyed now and counted on for all
eternity. Make sure you're trusting in the
right thing.

CHAPTER FOUR

God's Gift of Wealth

Pearl of Wisdom
"As for every man to whom God has given riches and wealth, and given him power to eat of it, to receive his heritage and rejoice in his labor—this is the gift of God."
Ecclesiastes 5:19

In the last chapter we looked at money from a negative perspective. According to God's Word, money can't satisfy. But there's another side to this coin (no pun intended). Solomon, the wealthiest man of his day, tells us that riches also can be seen as a gift from God. In fact, it's only how we sometimes misuse the wealth God gives us that brings a negative connotation to money. God is not against money; He is, however, against greed, gambling and other uses of money that destroy us.

Seventeen of the Lord's 36 parables have to do with property and stewardship. Clearly, this was an important subject to Jesus. The problem is we have a skewed understanding of what wealth is. The Funk & Wagnalls dictionary defines wealth as "A large aggregate of real and personal property, an abundance of those material or worldly things that men desire to possess." That definition catches the spirit of our times exactly.

We see wealth in terms of having an abundance of material or worldly things. Riches consist of how many cars you own or how many square feet are in your house. Take Bill Gates's home for example. Mr. Gates is the chairman of Microsoft and one of the wealthiest men in the world. When local city administrators toured Bill and Melinda Gates's house, they made a few comments about what they saw. They found, for example, 300 people working on the house while they were there, including 104 electricians. There were no visible electrical outlets anywhere (apparently Bill doesn't like the clutter). You climb 112 steps from the main floor to the main entry. Or if you want, you can take the elevator. The wood columns from the main floor to the roof in the entry area are more than 70 feet tall. The floor is heated everywhere, including the driveway and the walks.

Mr. Gates has a four-car garage. The house for the maintenance staff has its own three-car garage. If you want, music will follow you throughout the house, even to the bottom of the pool. Melinda has 42 linear feet of space in her closet for hanging clothes, all operated like a dry cleaner's rack. And, by the way, the master bathtub can be filled to the right temperature and the right depth by Mr. Gates as he drives home from work. The opulence of the Gates's mansion reflects the mentality we have today about wealth. The more we have, the more we spend.

When we get back to the Bible, however, we find that wealth is a lot more than money. Wealth is the sum total of all that God has given us. Genesis 13 makes it apparent in Abraham's day that wealth was defined by the number of cattle or the number of camels a person owned. Later on, wealth was determined by the amount of land that an individual owned (Josh. 17). In our society, possessions of all types determine wealth. Your computers, automobiles, sport utility vehicles, microwaves, VCRs, money market funds and all the other stuff you own constitute your wealth. But that's the definition of wealth in the mind of a flawed society. It doesn't take into account everything God has done. If we want to understand the truth about wealth, we need to take some other factors into consideration.

All wealth belongs to God

When we understand wealth as the gift of God, we understand that it comes from God and it belongs to God. This is a very difficult attitude for the world to adopt. But the Bible makes it clear that God created everything, God sustains everything and God owns everything. Psalm 104:24 declares, "The earth is full of Your possessions." In 1 Chronicles 29:11 we read, "Yours, O LORD, is the greatness, the power and the glory, the victory and the majesty; for all that is in heaven and in earth is Yours." Haggai 2:8 reminds us, "'The silver is Mine, and the gold is Mine,' says the LORD of Hosts." Everything in the ground, everything above the ground, everything in the air, everything that passes through the air ultimately belongs to God. He owns the cattle on a thousand hills, the wealth in every mine.

When we believe that wealth belongs to us, however, we get ourselves in trouble. We say, "It's mine, I earned it, I worked hard for it. It belongs to me, and I'll do with it whatever I want." If that's your attitude, you have been duped by Satan in a big way. Satan wants us to believe that everything we have belongs to us and we are not responsible to anyone for how we use it. But the truth is it's not ours; it's God's. Wealth is a stewardship from God. We are just holding God's wealth for Him, using what we need of it to live on, and investing the rest so that it will bring a greater yield to Him (Matt. 25:14-30). God wants to see what we'll do with it. So whether it's money, land or possessions, we will never be rightly related to what we have until we recognize that it is not ours. All that we have belongs to God.

Wealth is a gift from God

John Wesley said, "When the possessor of Heaven and Earth brought you into being and placed you in this world, He placed you here not as an owner but as a steward. As such, He entrusted you for a season with goods of various kinds. But the sole property of these still rests in Him nor can ever be alienated from Him, as you are not your own but His. Such as likewise all you enjoy."

Someone might say, "All right, that's John Wesley talking. After all, he was a preacher. He didn't have a big car. All he had was a horse. He didn't have much money. He traveled from place to place in virtual poverty. Maybe this is just sour grapes." But it's not. What John Wesley said comes directly out of the Bible. Wealth belongs to God and it is a gift to us. It's one of the pearls of wisdom that will guide us into the appropriate use of our finances. When God gives us the gift of wealth, even if it's just a tiny amount, He gives it to us to use for Him, not to hold onto tightly.

Ultimately, everything we have is a gift from God. In His grace, God shares His property with us. In His grace, God shares the ability for you and me to make money in order to put food on our table and to clothe our families. He owns everything. It's all because of His amazing grace that we enjoy any of what He owns.

Deuteronomy 8:1-8 says,

Every commandment which I command you today you must be careful to observe, that you may live and multiply, and go in and possess the land which the LORD swore to your fathers. And you shall remember that the LORD your God led you all the way these forty years in the wilderness, to humble you and test you, to know what was in your heart, whether you would keep His commandments or not.

So He humbled you, allowed you to hunger, and fed you with manna which you did not know nor did your fathers know, that He might make you know that man shall not live by bread alone; but man lives by every word that proceeds from the mouth of the LORD.

Your garments did not wear out on you, nor did your foot swell these forty years.

So you should know in your heart that as a man chastens his son, so the LORD your God chastens you.

Therefore you shall keep the commandments of the LORD your God, to walk in His ways and to fear Him.

For the LORD your God is bringing you into a good land, a land of brooks of water, of fountains and springs, that flow out with valleys and hills;

a land of wheat and barley, of vines and fig trees and pomegranates, a land of olive oil and honey."

It would be hard to misunderstand these verses. All that we enjoy in our lives is ultimately the gift of God to us. Instead of complaining that we do not have more, we would be wise to be grateful that we have as much as we do. Your home may not look much like Bill Gates's, but it is as much God's gift to you as your money is. Your family is as much God's gift to you as your income. Your church is as much God's gift to you as your bank account. The wealth of God comes in many and various forms, but it all comes from the gracious hand of God.

Don't brag about how much God gives you or complain about how little He gives you. All good things are measured out from His hand just as we need them. Those who have smaller homes or more meager bank accounts may find they have much greater riches in other areas of life, if only they could see them with thankful eyes.

Take heed to the warning

God gave Israel a great land. It was a land flowing with milk and honey. What a wonderful place for God to bring the Israelites after being slaves in Egypt for 430 years. But as we look further, we discover this warning in verses 11-14:

Beware that you do not forget the LORD your God by not keeping His commandments, His judgments, and His statutes which I command you today,

lest—when you have eaten and are full, and have built beautiful houses and dwell in them;

and when your herds and your flocks multiply, and your silver and your gold are multiplied, and all you have is multiplied;

when your heart is lifted up, and you forget the LORD your God who brought you out of the land of Egypt, from the house of bondage.

Warnings are for our good. If God were not a good God, He wouldn't take the time to warn us about those things that will destroy us. But God is so good that He gave this warning in verses 17-18:

Then you say in your heart, "My power and the might of my hand have gained me this wealth."

And you shall remember the LORD your God, for it is He who gives you power to get wealth, that He may establish His covenant which He swore to your fathers, as it is this day.

This pearl of wisdom is the same one found in Ecclesiastes 5:19. God gives us wonderful gifts. God gives us wealth. He gives us land. He gives us possessions, whether it's cattle or sheep, cars or diamonds. But we dare not forget the Giver.

But maybe you're thinking, *Wait a minute. I don't have any of these things.* That makes no difference, because our attitude toward our lack of wealth reveals our attitude toward God. If we see God as rich toward us, regardless of what property we have, we'll recognize that everything we do possess, even if it's just a little, is God's gift. If we have the attitude of gratitude, we will be grateful for a hundred dollars just as we would for a million. God is not bound by any law to give us anything; He is only bound by His own generous spirit, which desires to give us everything. When we view wealth from His perspective, we'll be eternally grateful.

The test of character

The real question we need to think about is, why does God give us this wealth? Does He give us this wealth to build large mansions? Does He give us these possessions to live in the lap of luxury? No, I don't think so. Remember the pearl of wisdom from Ecclesiastes 5:19. We receive our heritage and our labor as gifts from God, but He gives us these gifts as a test of our character.

Fred Smith, a Christian businessman, said it this way: "God entrusts us with money as a test, for like a toy to the child, it is training for handling things of more value." The way you handle the money that you have shows God what your character is like. It's an opportunity to demonstrate to God, to those around you, even to yourself, whether you have the character that reflects God or the kind that reflects greed.

Many people who have had money also have had great character. Mr. Welch of Welch's grape juice; J. C. Kraft of Kraft Cheese; Henry P. Kroll of Quaker Oats; William Colgate of the Colgate Soap Company; Walter Johnson, the founder of Holiday Inn; J. C. Penney of the J. C. Penney stores; and R. G. LeTourneau of LeTourneau University and all the LeTourneau equipment. These are men who put God first in their businesses. Starting out, they gave to God a tithe, maybe 15 percent. Some of them got up to 90 percent. But when you give back to God 90 percent of what He gives to you, what do you have left? Surprisingly, you don't have 10 percent left; you have it all left, because when you can pass the test of character, God knows He can entrust you with everything.

The great missionary statesman Hudson Taylor said, "Let us give up our work, our plans, ourselves, our lives, our loved ones, our influence, our rights into God's hand, and then when we have given all to Him there will be nothing left for us to be troubled about."

Are you spending all your time trying to save your wealth? Are you constantly seeking to find new and better ways to have bigger and better things? Then take this pearl of wisdom to heart, and it will keep you from financial ruin. Don't treat what money you have, whether it's a little or a lot, as your own. Treat it as God's and it won't buy things you don't need. Treat it as God's and it won't rule your life. If you treat it as God's, you'll discover that it will go a lot further than it does now.

Everything you have is God's gift to you. What you do with everything God gives you is your gift to Him. Is your life all about getting or all about giving?

CHAPTER FIVE

Investing in the Future

Pearl of Wisdom
"Cast your bread upon the waters, for you
will find it after many days."
Ecclesiastes 11:1

A man was crossing by foot a barren area in the western part of the United States and was nearly dead from thirst. Unexpectedly, he stumbled across an old, deserted shack with a hand pump out front. At the base of the pump someone had left a tightly sealed jug of water with a note attached. The note read, "Don't drink this water. Use it to prime the pump. Refill it for the next person." The man hesitated. He was terribly thirsty and, if by chance the well was dry, he would be pouring out his only opportunity for survival. Finally he decided to take a chance. Slowly he poured the water down the pump and worked the handle. As the last of the life-giving liquid was going down the pipe, up gushed a plentiful supply of fresh water. When the man departed, he left a full jug of water and reattached the note. But he added the words, "Try it. It worked for me."

Solomon offered the same pearl of wisdom: if you want to drink from the well, you first must prime the pump. This passage is about sowing and investing, giving out and having the faith that God will give back to you in return—someday, if not immediately. That's why Solomon says, "Cast your bread upon the waters, and you will find it after many days."

The Turks have a similar proverb: "Do good, throw it into the water. If the fish doesn't know it, God does." The idea is that giving is living, living in a way that's honoring to God. Here's how it's done.

Give without regard for rewards

Casting your bread upon the waters is not a give-to-get scheme. Notice that Ecclesiastes 11:1 does not say, "Cast your bread upon the waters today, and God will bring back tenfold tonight." It's true that such verses as Proverbs 3:9-10 say, "Honor the LORD with your possessions, and with the firstfruits of all your increase; so your barns will be filled with plenty, and your vats will overflow with new wine." And frequently in God's Word the Lord promises that when we give, He will respond by blessing us. But *why* we give is just as important as *what* we give, and often even more so.

We do not give in order to get. The statement in Luke 6:38, "Give, and it will be given to you: good measure, pressed down, shaken together, and running over," is a promise of blessing, not the purpose for giving. We don't give to get in return; we give because it's good to give. When we exercise responsible giving, God exercises bountiful blessing.

The word *give* appears more than 1,000 times in the Bible. Obviously, God considers giving very important. Proverbs 13:7 warns, "There is one who makes himself rich, yet has nothing; and one who makes himself poor, yet has great riches." In other words, the person who focuses on getting ends up ultimately with nothing, while the one who majors on giving will have an abundance. The Bible says that when we give, God may make us wealthy, but it may be in ways we could never dream. Giving makes us rich, but we may have little cash to show for it. So why do we give? Why do we cast our bread upon the waters? We do it because it's right!

A well-known German preacher of the 17th century named August Francke founded an orphanage and took in homeless children right off the streets in Halle, Germany. One day when he was desperately in need of funds to carry on his work, a destitute Christian widow came to his door begging for money. All she wanted was one gold *duckte*. Because of his own financial situation, he politely but regretfully had to refuse. He just didn't have it to give to her. Disheartened, this woman sat down and began to weep.

Francke was so moved by her tears he said, "Wait a minute. Let me go in and talk to the Lord about this." He went into the orphanage, closed the door to his office and began to pray, seeking God's guidance. As he prayed, he felt the Spirit of God wanted him to give that woman his last gold coin. Trusting the Lord to meet his own needs, he gave her the money. He had no anticipation of anything in response; he just did what was right.

Two mornings later he received a very warm letter of thanks from this widow. She wrote that because of his generosity she had asked the Lord to shower the orphanage with gifts. That same day he received 12 gold coins from a rich woman, and 2 from a friend in Sweden. He thought that he had been amply rewarded for his good deed to this woman, but shortly after that he was informed that Prince Ludwig von Vertenberg had died, and in his will he had directed that 500 gold pieces be given to the orphanage.

This is the attitude that God looks for among His people. He wants us to cast our bread upon the waters, to give without regard to rewards. That pearl of wisdom teaches us simply to do what is right and let God take care of the rest. I'm sure August Francke would say, "Try it. It worked for me."

It also has worked for Back to the Bible. As you may know, for many years our ministry has been helping deserving students get a Bible education in countries outside of North America so they can be better equipped to serve the Lord. We do this through our International Scholarship Fund. Many friends and supporters of Back to the Bible have contributed to this fund, from which we award partial scholarships to students who remain in their country, or travel to a neighboring country, to train for ministry.

Almost two decades ago, we received a scholarship application from a married student with a young family. David Logacho had been an engineer at a NASA tracking station but felt God was calling him to full-time ministry. He wanted to attend a Bible school in Latin America and return to his native Ecuador to serve the Lord. He met all the qualifications for the scholarship, and he received it. We had never met this young man or his family, but we invested in his future.

Some years later, our director for Back to the Bible in Latin America, who also was the Bible teacher on our program *La Biblia Dice . . . (The Bible Says . . .)*, went to be with the Lord. We formed a search committee to ask God to lead us to His choice for a new Bible teacher and director. God led us to David Logacho, who today is heard on 180 stations throughout Central and South America, teaching the Word in Spanish daily just as I do in English. All of that came about because one day Back to the Bible decided to give a scholarship to a young man. When you cast your bread upon the water, you don't expect such a return. You simply do it because it is right. Yet when we do what is right, God takes care of us. That's one of the great pearls of wisdom from the Book of Ecclesiastes.

Give without regard to adversity

A traveling salesman got off his route one day and was lost on a side road. After driving awhile on a narrow, winding road, he came upon a farmer sitting on the front porch of his old, dilapidated house. The farmer was kind of rough looking, with ragged clothes and bare feet. After the man asked for directions back to the main road, he decided to engage the farmer in some small talk. So the salesman asked, "How's your cotton doing this year?" "Ain't got none," replied the farmer. "Afraid of boll weevils." "How about your corn crop?" the salesman asked. "How's it doing?" Again the farmer said, "Didn't plant any. Feared it'd be too dry." "Well," the salesman continued, "how about your potatoes? Are you having a good year for potatoes?" "Nope," said the farmer, "didn't plant any 'taters either. Scared of 'tater bugs." "What did you plant?" the salesman questioned. "Nothin'," the farmer replied. "I jest played it safe."

Some Christians are like that. They just want to play it safe. They've heard of a huge economic crisis coming and they want to be ready for it. Or they want to make sure they have enough money invested for retirement. Who knows how much is enough? Some want to be sure that if they give, it won't inconvenience them later on. But Solomon says in Ecclesiastes 11:4, "He who observes the wind will not sow, and he who regards the clouds will not reap." In other words, cast your bread upon the waters without regard to adversity.

I'm not suggesting you shouldn't prepare for the future. Careful preparation is a biblical concept (Prov. 6:6-8; 30:25). But too many Christians are giving far too little to the Lord's work now simply because they lack the faith in God to believe He will meet their needs in the future. If the coming economic crisis doesn't come, or if you do not live to see it come, will you be better off casting your bread upon the water and trusting God, or hoarding your wealth in an attempt to hedge against hard times? Isn't

God still God during the hard times as well as the good times?

Certainly, sometimes it's more difficult to give than it is at other times. But if you wait for that perfect time to give, chances are you won't give at all. Eternity is rapidly approaching. Cast your bread upon the waters without regard to adversity, because it's the right thing to do, not because it's the easy thing to do.

Give without regard to time

In verse 6 we're told, "In the morning sow your seed, and in the evening do not withhold your hand; for you do not know which will prosper, either this or that, or whether both alike will be good." Solomon is saying, "You need to cast your bread upon the waters without regard to time."

Sometimes we cast our bread upon the waters when we're young. We invest in our own future and the ministry God will give us. Lots of people have done that by pursuing an education. Many have used the years of their youth to learn skills that they're now using for the Lord. That's casting your bread upon the waters while it's still morning.

But don't miss this. Casting your bread is not a youthful activity only. You also should cast your bread upon the waters even when you're older. In my mind, there are two reasons for casting when you're older.

First, you don't know how many years God has left for you. There may still be plenty of things He wants you to do. Therefore you've got to stay in shape spiritually and you need to keep up with technology. You need to prepare as if you had half your life left. But second, you should cast your bread upon the waters in your older years because it is unlikely that you do have half your life left. Your time is growing short. Your later years are an important time to make an investment in the future, especially in the work of the Lord, because your opportunities become more rare. Remember, what you invest in eternity lasts forever; what you invest in time will only last a few years. Don't be shortsighted. Solomon says, "In the evening do not withhold your hand."

Investing in the future

Here's the great pearl of wisdom from this verse. God calls us to cast our bread upon the waters and let Him bring the return. In essence, He asks us to invest in the future, not knowing exactly what the future holds, and not really expecting anything to come back to us. Is that wise? Like a fox it's wise. It's doing what's right, even though no one may know except God. But He is the great rewarder. He keeps accurate accounts. He pays the highest possible dividend on investments. He wants you to benefit to the fullest extent possible from casting your bread.

Lots of people read good Christian books, listen to Christian programs and get great benefit from Christian resources, but they never give anything back. They never cast their bread upon the waters. They're looking for what feeds them, but they have no concept of the importance of investing in others. But to conclude where we began, it's like priming that old pump. You've got to pour some water in if you're going to get some water out.

If the thirsty traveler in the desert can trust a sign left to him by a fellow traveler, you can trust a pearl of wisdom left to you by a fellow traveler. Solomon said, "Cast, and it will come back." It's the nature of God to make promises and then make good on His promises. What you invest in time benefits you in time. What you invest in eternity benefits you in time and eternity. Doesn't it seem strange that we cling so tightly to our "bread" when God's pearl of wisdom counsels us to let it fly? Cast your bread. Try it, and you'll find it works.

CHAPTER SIX

All for One

Pearl of Wisdom
"Though one may be overpowered by anoth-
er, two can withstand him. And a threefold
cord is not quickly broken."
Ecclesiastes 4:12

In October 1997, a freak snowstorm hit Lincoln, Nebraska. This was early for snow-fall in our part of the country and the leaves were still on the trees. Excessively heavy, wet snow fell within 24 hours. The official total accumulation at the airport was 13 inches, but most of the city recorded much more. I had 20 inches of snow in my backyard. The massive weight of the white stuff caused roofs to cave in and broke tree limbs like they were matchsticks. More than 50,000 trees in the city were lost. By itself, a single snowflake wouldn't have been noticed. To-gether, they brought a bustling city to a standstill for almost a week.

This is a perfect example of the pearl of wisdom Solomon is sharing here in Ecclesi-astes 4:12. On our own we can accomplish a limited amount, but united with others we're unbeatable. "Though one may be overpowered by another, two can withstand him. And a threefold cord is not quickly broken."

This pearl has special reference to the church. Every local assembly should demonstrate the unity of a threefold cord. It's our unity that brings strength to the church. It's our unity that God uses as a weapon against the united forces of evil. Unity is of God, and it should be characterized by at least four qualities.

Diversity

Unity does not mean uniformity, although some things must be the same. The entire church, for example, needs to know the same Lord and Master, Jesus Christ. It is obvious, too, that the congregation needs to be pulling in the same direction. But this still leaves a lot of room for diversity.

Think about the strands of a cord. To be strong, those strands don't have to be the same color or texture or material. They simply have to work together for a common purpose. Think about the local church. Members have individual personalities and characteristics. We are young and we are old. We are from different ethnic and racial backgrounds. Our strength is enhanced by our diversity. What one has to contribute, another may not. But in diversity each one brings to the church something that God wants it to be. The Bible says that we need the diversity of gifts in order to have the kind of church God wants us to have (1 Cor. 12:14-21).

I remember years ago when my daughters were in their early teen years, it was popular for kids to wear friendship bracelets. A friendship bracelet was just a little cord, maybe pieces of different-colored yarn tightly woven together, that the teens would wear on their wrists to remind them of another friend. My daughters would exchange these friendship bracelets with their best friends and thus identify with those closest to them.

When I saw these friendship bracelets for the first time on my daughters' arms and I questioned what they were, you should have seen the looks on their faces. "Come on, Dad, get with it. Don't you understand this? This is a friendship bracelet." They didn't look like much (in fact, to me they looked pretty awful), but the bracelets were very meaningful to my girls because of the diversity of friends they had.

The writers of the Bible, some 40 of them, were also very diverse people. God knew that a diverse group of people, from sheepherders to kings, would be able to present the Gospel better than if He committed it to only one or two personalities. Aren't you glad that Amos, the herdsman from Tekoa, was paired with Moses, the fiery emancipator of Israel? And Peter, the epitome of impulsiveness, was paired with John, the sensitive disciple? How rich the styles of the Bible are because of God's wisdom to bring unity out of diversity. That's as true today as it was when the Bible was written. At a worldwide ministry like Back to the Bible, I know that unity in diversity is important. I am not the only Bible teacher at Back to the Bible. In fact, we have more than 40 Bible teachers worldwide, and they are a very diverse group of people. Collectively, they speak about 20 languages and teach the Word ably to a large portion of the world.

Here in Lincoln, I need a diverse group of people to help me conduct my ministry every day. I need recording engineers, writers, people who answer telephones, people who enter data into computers, pressmen who print books, television camera operators—people who do all the things God gifts them to do, because it takes a lot of people to reach the world with the Gospel. We all are diverse in our backgrounds and gifts, but we are unified in our purpose of leading men and women into a dynamic relationship with God. This is the kind of diversity that can bring great blessings in the church, in our ministries and in our lives.

To impact the people around us, we don't need uniformity, but we do need unity. We can enjoy diversity and still change the world. But we can't impact the world without unity.

Cooperation

The lack of cooperation among God's people is so evident it is troubling. Someone once described the response of a group of thoroughbred horses to danger versus that of a group of mules. The thoroughbreds gather in a circle with their heads inward and their back hooves facing outward. As the source of danger draws close, they kick out with their hooves and drive it away. The mules, on the other hand, form a circle with their heads out and their hindquarters facing inward. When they kick, they only kick each other. In your experience, does the church more often resemble mules or thoroughbreds?

There must be cooperation in the church. If there is no cooperation, there is no unity; and if there is no unity, there is no strength. As the church meets each weekend, we desperately need cooperation between the pulpit and the pews, as well as between those who occupy the pews. This is what the apostle Paul begged of the believers in the church at Corinth. First Corinthians 1:10 says, "Now I plead with you, brethren, by the name of our Lord Jesus Christ, that you all speak the same thing, and that there be no divisions among you, but that you be perfectly joined together in the same mind and in the same judgment." Immediately Paul takes them to task for their lack of cooperation: "For it has been declared to me concerning you, my brethren, by those of Chloe's household, that there are contentions among you. Now I say this, that each of you says, 'I am of Paul,' or 'I am of Apollos,' or 'I am of Cephas,' or 'I am of Christ'" (vv. 11-12). Then Paul asks these questions, "Is Christ divided? Was Paul crucified for you? Or were you baptized in the name of Paul?" (v. 13).

What is the apostle saying? Simply put, diversity is good, but it demands unity; and if there's going to be unity, there must be cooperation.

The Corinthian believers were acting like a group of mules. They were not cooperating with each other. In fact, in chapter 3 of this same book, Paul writes,

> And I, brethren, could not speak to you as to spiritual people but as to carnal, as to babes in Christ. I fed you with milk and not with solid food; for until now you were not able to receive it, and even now you are still not able; for you are still carnal. For where there

are envy, strife, and divisions among you, are you not carnal and behaving like mere men? For when one says, "I am of Paul," and another, "I am of Apollos," are you not carnal? Who then is Paul, and who is Apollos, but ministers through whom you believed, as the Lord gave to each one? I planted, Apollos watered, but God gave the increase (vv. 1-6).

Paul's point is pretty clear. For a cord to be strong, there has to be cooperation among the strands.

When all the strands are cooperating, we can accomplish amazing feats. In a little town in north central Nebraska, there was a barn that had a problem. It was Herman Ostrey's barn, and it was under 29 inches of water because of a rising creek. Herman needed to get his barn moved off of that foundation to a new foundation that he'd poured 143 feet away. There was one slight problem—the barn weighed 17,000 pounds. Herman Ostrey's son Mike devised a latticework of steel tubing that he nailed, bolted and welded to both the inside and the outside of the barn. To this steel tubing he attached hundreds of handles. After one practice lift, 344 volunteers picked up the 17,000-pound barn and walked the structure up a slight incline, each of them supporting less than 50 pounds. Within three minutes that barn was on its new foundation. That's cooperation!

Just imagine what the Body of Christ could accomplish if in our diversity and our unity there was real cooperation. If each of us was only willing to pick up a few pounds of that 17,000-pound barn, we could carry it too. More to the point, if each of us carried the Gospel to one neighbor or family member, given enough of us, we could reach the world with the message of Christ in no time flat. That's a real pearl of wisdom.

Strength

One of my favorite fables comes from the famous Aesop. He told about an old man who, at the point of death, summoned his sons together. He wanted to give them some parting advice. He ordered one of his servants to bring a bundle of sticks, and he said to his eldest son, "Break it." The son strained and he strained, but with all of his efforts he was unable to break the bundle. The other sons tried as well, and they too were unsuccessful. Then the father said, "Untie the sticks and each of you take one." When they had done so, he called out to them and said, "Break it," and each son broke his stick easily.

Aesop's fable illustrates this pearl of wisdom from Ecclesiastes. Together we have more strength than we have individually. The bag of sticks tied together could not be broken by any of the sons, but when their unity was disbanded, one by one they were easily broken. There is inherent strength in unity.

When it comes to a three-stranded cord, each strand has to carry its own weight. But what happens if one strand fails? There are still two other strands to carry the load. That's the kind of strength you cannot possibly get from a single strand of rope.

Exodus 17 records the battle between Joshua's Israelite forces and the Amalekites. This is one of the great examples of strength in unity in the Bible. This passage depicts Joshua, the great military leader, and Moses, the great intercessor. Exodus 17:8-13 says,

Now Amalek came and fought with Israel in Rephidim. And Moses said to Joshua, "Choose us some men and go out, fight with Amalek. Tomorrow I will stand on the top of the hill with the rod of God in my hand." So Joshua did as Moses said to him, and fought with Amalek. And Moses, Aaron, and Hur went up to the top of the hill. And so it was, when Moses held up his hand, that Israel prevailed; and when he let down his hand, Amalek prevailed. But Moses' hands became heavy; so they took a stone and put it under him, and he sat on it. And Aaron and Hur supported his hands, one on one side, and the other on the other side; and his hands were steady until the going down of the sun. So Joshua defeated Amalek and his people with the edge of the sword.

This story is the perfect example of cooperation, unity and diversity. Three different men, with different personalities, different ages, different abilities, all working together to insure Joshua's victory. But more than cooperation, unity and diversity, this is a story about strength. Where did Moses get his strength? He got it from the cooperation of Aaron and Hur holding up his arms. A threefold cord is not quickly broken because of its strength.

If Satan can take the church apart, he can easily break us one by one. If he can splinter the local church, we will easily be defeated. In fact, the Devil is counting on our being fractured and factionalized. It's one of his major strategies. That's why we must be unified like a threefold cord: our strength will keep us together.

Effort

But there's one last aspect to this pearl of wisdom that we want to explore—a threefold cord implies effort. Each one works harder because they know the others are also working.

I recently read a story about a man whose car slid off the road and ended up in a ditch. A farmhouse was nearby, so the man went up to the door and asked the owner if he had a tractor and could pull his car out of the ditch. "Well," the farmer said, "I don't have a tractor, but I do have an old mule named Blue." The man replied, "I doubt if that mule is strong enough to pull my car out of the ditch." The farmer just laughed and said, "Oh, you don't know Blue. He's a proud mule." So Blue was hitched to the car and the farmer said, "Pull, Blue!" But the car didn't move. And then the farmer called out, "Pull, Elmer!" And the car still didn't move. And then the farmer yelled out, "Pull, Biscuit!" Suddenly the car was freed and pulled up over the embankment to the road.

The owner of the car thanked the farmer for what he did, and then he said, "Before I go I have one question. You called your mule by three different names. Why did you did that?" And the farmer said, "Oh, that's simple. You see, Blue is blind. At first he figured he was the only one pulling. But when he thought there were two others pulling with him, he pulled harder."

Have you experienced the same thing? I have. The harder I work here at Back to the Bible, the harder people around me work. And the harder they work, the harder I work. That's the way it ought to be. We should recognize that we're in this together, and because we are, each of us gives more effort than if we worked by ourselves. If you were the only person in your church, you probably wouldn't work very hard. But you're not alone. You're part of a threefold cord pulling together. That knowledge empowers us to work harder and put forth greater effort.

Here is a pearl of wisdom from the Book of Ecclesiastes. It's much tougher to break a threefold cord than it is to break three separate cords. Working together always accomplishes more than working singularly. A threefold cord teaches us about unity—a unity characterized by diversity, cooperation, strength and effort. When we work by ourselves, Satan watches and sometimes smiles. But when we all work together, Satan trembles. And his fear is justified. He knows there isn't anything we can't do by the Spirit of God when we do it as a threefold cord.

CHAPTER SEVEN

Dead Flies

Pearl of Wisdom
"Dead flies putrefy the perfumer's ointment,
and cause it to give off a foul odor;
so does a little folly to one respected
for wisdom and honor."
Ecclesiastes 10:1

Companies that make computer software usually find that every new program they produce initially has some "bugs" in it. These are little glitches that cause the program not to work the way it ought. If the program is to be successful, these bugs have to be worked out. No one wants to use a faulty computer program.

Solomon was concerned about different but equally disastrous bugs. These were the bugs that got into the ointment used to make perfumes. Often in the Middle East people would perfume their bodies as a way to enhance personal hygiene and please the senses. Spices, brought by camel caravan from the Far East or Egypt, would be mixed with oils to create pleasing and sometimes exotic perfumes. One nasty little fly, however, could fall into a jar of perfumer's ointment and cause the whole mixture to smell foul.

But Solomon also gives a spiritual twist to this problem and in doing so provides one of life's lasting pearls of wisdom. Literally Ecclesiastes 10:1 says that the "flies of death" cause perfumed oil to stink. And what dead flies do to perfumed oil, a moment of foolishness does to those who are ordinarily characterized by wisdom and honor.

The New American Standard version translates this verse, "Dead flies make a perfumer's oil stink, so a little foolishness is weightier than wisdom and honor." As one pesky little bug can ruin an otherwise pleasant-smelling perfume, so one foolish act can outweigh all the good in an otherwise godly life. Remembering that pearl of wisdom can change your life.

Nobody likes flies. We don't like to think about the possibility that a single pesky fly could ruin a moment, ruin our day or maybe even ruin the future. So we have to do something about those flies, especially if they're spiritual ones.

What are some of these flies in the ointment of our lives? What is it that causes a stench to rise to the nostrils of God, instead of the sweet smell of perfumed ointment? In all likelihood, we could find a little fly that corresponds to every letter of the alphabet, a sin that is a dead fly that dirties the ointment of our lies. But let's be content with just the first three—the ABCs of smelly sins—that can soil a Christian's life in a hurry.

Adultery

Big A, little d-u-l-t-e-r-y. That spells adultery. We don't even use the word much anymore. Today people "live together" or they "have an affair," all of which sound pretty innocuous. But the word *adultery* more accurately describes a dead fly that polutes far too many lives. Almost no fly causes a more putrefying smell than this one, the "A fly." Adultery not only leads to misery and pain and frequently to divorce, it also destroys a Christian's testimony and brings reproach on the name of the Savior.

Interestingly, when God issued His Ten Commandments to Moses on Mount Sinai, two of the ten related to the sexuality between men and women. Commandment seven says, "You shall not commit adultery," and commandment ten states, "You shall not covet your neighbor's wife" (Ex. 20:14, 17). Those are clear commands of God. Adultery is *always* unacceptable. In God's eyes adultery is always sin, regardless of how commonly it is portrayed on TV, or how titillating it is written about in magazines, or how widespread it is in society. God still says that adultery is a dead fly that dirties your life. No one ever commits adultery with the approval of God.

Proverbs 6:32 says, "Whoever commits adultery with a woman lacks understanding; he who does so destroys his own soul." In John 8, when Jesus encountered the woman caught in adultery, He used the occasion to show the Pharisees their sin of hypocrisy. At the same time, however, He did not condone the woman's sin. In fact, so strong was Jesus' teaching on adultery that He told another group of Pharisees, "Whoever divorces his wife, except for sexual immorality, and marries another, commits adultery; and whoever marries her who is divorced commits adultery" (Matt. 19:9).

Those are pretty strong words, but then, Jesus knew how many people would be hurt with the pain of infidelity. The Savior wants us all to understand just how horrible adultery is.

Whether it's your life or the life of another, adultery always destroys. It destroys your purity, your integrity, your relationships. It destroys your family. It can destroy your children. Yet look around you. Adultery is the norm, not the exception. In the United States, for example, living with a person for an extended period of time, either prior to marriage or in place of marriage, is now an acceptable and widespread practice. Among people who get married this year, more than six out of ten will have lived together. Cohabitation in America has increased a whopping 443 percent since 1970. And the fastest increase has been in the last three years, where cohabitation has jumped 1,882 percent. That's a lot of dead flies making a lot of dirty ointment. Yet no one seems to care—except God.

One of the things that destroys our lives quicker than anything else, one of the dead flies that can take a perfumed life and make it smell horrible, is when we're unfaithful to our spouse. Adultery is never acceptable to God. It's one of the fastest ways to make your life stink. The best way to avert this smelly practice is to avoid any and all situations that could tempt you to become enamored with someone else.

If you feel affections growing toward someone who is not your spouse, here are three simple yet very effective ways to keep from smelling up your life. First, if you can, avoid the person to whom you're attracted. Don't go near him or her and never be alone with that person. Second, ask God to throttle your passions and take these illicit affections away from you. He can and will do that. Third, increase your heart affections and open appreciation for your spouse by every legitimate means available to you. Be genuine in your love for your spouse.

Satan is the source of dead flies and smelly ointment. God is the source of fidelity in marriage. Do not become one of Satan's fools and society's statistics. Be a man or woman of God instead.

Bitterness

The second of our alphabet bugs, the "B fly," is bitterness. Sometimes we don't see this as significant as the sin of adultery, but often it's the bitterness between husbands and wives that pushes them into adultery. Bitterness is not something we ought to minimize. It's a deadly fly. When you harbor bitterness toward your mate, your children, your parents, your pastor or your neighbors, it can destroy your life.

In Acts 8, when Peter confronted Simon Magus, who wanted to buy the power of the Holy Spirit, he said, "Repent therefore of this your wickedness, and pray God if perhaps the thought of your heart may be forgiven you" (v. 22). But Peter went on to say, "For I see that you are poisoned by bitterness and bound by iniquity" (v. 23). Don't miss the tandem that Peter used: "Poisoned by bitterness and bound by iniquity." Bitterness is linked with iniquity, and together they poison and bind. That shows us just how dirty the perfume of life can become when it's stained by the dead fly of bitterness.

If your life is somehow bound by iniquity, the chances are pretty good that you were at one time poisoned by bitterness. That's why bitterness is so devastating. It may seem like a trivial matter, but bitterness can ruin your life. It is one of the deadliest flies that spoils the perfumer's ointment.

In Ephesians 4:30 Paul urges, "Do not grieve the Holy Spirit of God, by whom you were sealed for the day of redemption." How do we grieve the Holy Spirit? We don't have to wonder. Paul continues in the next verse to list some of the sins that grieve Him. Take special note of what tops the list: "Let all bitterness, wrath, anger, clamor, and evil speaking be put away from you, with all malice. And be kind to one another, tenderhearted, forgiving one another, just as God in Christ also forgave you" (vv. 31-32).

Knowing the damage that results from bitterness, is it any wonder Paul put it at the head of the list? The writer of Hebrews adds, "Pursue peace with all men, and holiness, . . . lest any root of bitterness springing up cause trouble, and by this many become defiled" (12:14-15). Again, it's hard not to notice the linkage between bitterness and defilement. With Simon in Acts 8, it was the poison of bitterness and the binding of iniquity. Here it's bitterness springing up and causing defilement. It should be obvious that bitterness is a deadly poison that can ruin our lives.

If you have any bitterness, it's smelling up your life. It's a deadly thing. It will ruin you in a different way than adultery will, but it will ruin you nonetheless. You need to unload that bitterness and rid yourself of it. But how? Here's what the Bible says. First, find out what is causing you to be bitter. Identify it honestly. Is it an impaired relationship with your family? Is it jealousy over someone at work? Is it because you didn't receive the recognition you thought you deserved? If you're honest with yourself, you'll have no difficulty identifying the source of your bitterness.

Then, once you've discovered what is causing you to be bitter, take it to Jesus Christ. Drop it at His feet. Confess your bitterness for what it is—sin. Apply the 1 John 1:9 principle to this dead fly. "If we confess our sins"—in this case, bitterness— "He is faithful and just to forgive us our sins and to cleanse us from all unrighteousness."

Finally, bury your bitterness. Don't let it surface again. The only way to bury it is to go to the one against whom you have been bitter, swallow your pride, confess your bitter feelings and ask for forgiveness. This way you unburden yourself, you please God and you win back your brother (Matt. 18:15). It's not easy, but it's the only thing that works.

Bitterness is a pesky fly. It ruins a lot of perfumed ointment, and none of us is immune from it. We all must take a big swat at this fly and see that we squash it as soon as we become aware of it, and then properly dispose of it.

Criticism
Adultery and bitterness are dead flies that

can wreak havoc in your life, but so can criticism. This "C fly" is one of those things that apparently people think is more blessed to give than to receive. At least, there's a lot of it going around.

Anyone who is in the public eye should expect criticism. *Back to the Bible* is heard on hundreds of stations by millions of listeners worldwide, and we receive many letters, phone calls and e-mail messages every day. I'm happy to say that a great majority of them are very positive, but not all. We are open to criticism just like anyone else. I have learned three little lessons about criticism from being criticized. Let me pass them on to you. Perhaps they will help you pick the dead flies of criticism out of your life.

First, all of us are frequently deserving of criticism, and we should expect to be criticized. I know that's true of me. But if as a Christian I'm not mature enough to take criticism, I'm not mature enough to handle praise either. Justified criticism, given from a heart of compassion that wants to help and not harm, should always be acceptable to the believer. We may not always like it, but it is good for us.

Second, even though we're frequently deserving of criticism, there will be times when we're criticized that we don't deserve it. I learned early on as a Christian leader that some people find it a whole lot easier to grumble about what's being done than to get out and do something on their own. Some folks never do anything for the Lord, but feel compelled to criticize those who do. Perhaps they consider criticism their spiritual gift. In spite of this, I have found that it's better to be unjustly criticized by people who are in error than to be justly criticized because I am in error.

Third, criticism is far more likely to be beneficial if it's given with a compliment. I'm always baffled by people who never write to say how they have benefited by a *Back to the Bible* broadcast or never financially assist our ministry, but who feel they must write to be critical. Such criticism dirties the ointment more quickly than any other kind.

Here is a genuine pearl of wisdom. You can have the most fragrant perfume ever made, but one little fly can ruin it. You can have the most admirable life ever lived, but one little sin can ruin it. Dead flies destroy good perfume. They give a foul odor to even a beautiful fragrance.

What about you today? Are there little things that are destroying your life—foul flies that make the rest of your good life smell a bit? Now is the time to do something about them. Turn to the Lord and tell Him what it is that's smelling up your life. Then, seek His forgiveness for the dead flies you've allowed to dirty the ointment of your life. Finally, implement a "dead fly maintenance program." Through daily confession, prayer and reading God's Word, keep your ointment clean and sweet smelling. All who are near you will be glad you did, and so will you.

CHAPTER EIGHT

A Good Name

Pearl of Wisdom
"A good name is better
than precious ointment."
Ecclesiastes 7:1

The infamous break-in at the Watergate Hotel was one of the saddest incidents in U.S. politics. Things were falling apart around the White House. Chaos reigned in the Oval Office. Shortly thereafter some of the White House staff were convicted and sent to prison. John Mitchell, one of the former members of the Nixon administration, was one of them. After serving his time and being released from prison, Mitchell made this astute observation: "Not much more can happen to you after you lose your reputation and your wife."

The former attorney general was right. Losing your wife is a great misfortune, but equally disastrous is losing your reputation. John Mitchell had lost both. How much better off he would have been if only he had heeded one of the great pearls of wisdom from the Book of Ecclesiastes: "A good name is better than precious ointment."

If I were to mention certain names to you, immediately your mind would conjure up certain images. Some would be positive images, some negative. For example, if I say Abraham Lincoln, how do you respond?

How about Attila the Hun, Winston Churchill or Adolph Hitler? Whether the images we have are good or bad, they all arise from a person's reputation.

In this pearl of wisdom, the Hebrew word translated "precious" means "joyful, good or cheerful," and the word for "ointment" literally means "an oil or a grease." Put together, the two Hebrew words could be translated "joyful oil." When the people of the ancient Near East were perfumed with oil, it was a symbol of joy and prosperity. Ecclesiastes 9:8 says, "Let your garments always be white, and let your head lack no oil." Solomon isn't talking about greasy hair; he's talking about the joy of having precious oil poured over your head.

Job wistfully remembered the days of his prosperity and joy with these words: "Oh, that I were as in months past . . . just as I was in the days of my prime, . . . when my steps were bathed with cream, and the rock poured out rivers of oil for me!" (Job 29:2, 4, 6).

But perfumed oil or ointment was also a metaphor for a reputation. The Song of Solomon begins with the beloved Shulamite saying of Solomon, "Let him kiss me with the kisses of his mouth—for your love is better than wine. Because of the fragrance of your good ointments, your name is ointment poured forth; therefore the virgins love you" (1:2-3). The pleasing aroma of Solomon's good name made him even more attractive to his beloved.

In this pearl of wisdom from Ecclesiastes 7:1, Solomon was not talking about dousing your head with oil and smelling better; he was talking about your good name. Your name represents your character or reputation. It's far better to be remembered with a good reputation than to enjoy the benefits of perfumed oil all the days of your life.

Unfortunately, it doesn't take much to ruin your reputation. You may spend a whole lifetime building it, but you can destroy it in a few unguarded moments. Think about all the people in the Bible whose names were tarnished by a single lapse in their character. Doubting Thomas is a prime example.

Doubting Thomas

Apart from being listed with the other disciples, Thomas is mentioned only three times in the Bible. In John 11:16, his name appears in the context of the death of Lazarus. Jesus was talking about going to Bethany when Thomas said to the other disciples, "Let us go also that we may die with Him." Thomas didn't have a death wish. He was just showing his great devotion to the Lord Jesus. In essence Thomas said, "Hey, let's go with Jesus. If it means that we die with Him, that's okay." Thomas was a man of great devotion. Does he sound like a doubter here?

The second time we encounter Thomas is in John 14:5. Jesus told His disciples He was going away and that they all knew where He was going. Everybody wondered what the Savior meant. Thomas voiced the question for the others. Essentially he said, "We don't have a clue where You're going. How would we know? You haven't told us."

The third time Thomas is mentioned in Scripture is in John 20:24-25. After Jesus' resurrection, He appeared first to Mary Magdalene in the garden and then later that night to the disciples assembled together. But Thomas was not present, so when the other disciples told him they had seen the risen Savior, in essence he said, "I'll believe, but I won't believe unless I see. Certain conditions have to be met. I'll lay down the conditions and then I'll believe. Until I see His hands, the print of the mark, and put my fingers into the print of the nails, and put my hand into His side, I will not believe."

The others believed that Jesus was alive, but they believed because they had seen Him. Thomas had not. Was he asking for any greater benefit than the other disciples already had? He would not believe without seeing Jesus alive, but neither had the other disciples.

These are the only three times Thomas is singled out for mention in the Bible. And what is it that you and I remember of him? Not his great devotion or his asking for clarification from the Savior. We remember his desire for physical proof before he would believe Jesus was alive. We remember his reputation as Doubting Thomas. Thomas's character was tarnished by one little lapse that, in context, may not have been so great a lapse after all.

Denying Peter

Then there's our good friend Peter, one of the premier characters of the New Testament. Peter again and again stood out for his boldness, his confidence and his preaching of the Word. It was Peter from whom Jesus won the greatest confession of faith of all time: "You are the Christ, the Son of the living God" (Matt. 16:16). Peter was the recognized leader of the disciples. He was one of those who boldly said to the high priest, "We ought to obey God rather than men" (Acts 5:29). But Peter made one dramatic mistake. When Jesus warned His friend that Peter would deny Him, he objected. "Even if I have to die with You, I will not deny You!" (Matt. 26:35). His promise was genuine—he just didn't keep it.

John 18:15-17, 25-27 records,

And Simon Peter followed Jesus, and so did another disciple. Now that disciple was known to the high priest, and went with Jesus into the courtyard of the high priest. But Peter stood at the door outside. Then the other disciple, who was known to the high priest, went out and spoke to her who kept the door, and brought Peter in. Then the servant girl who kept the door said to Peter, "You are not also one of this Man's disciples, are you?" He said, "I am not." . . . Now Simon Peter stood and warmed himself. Therefore they said unto him, "You are not also one of His disciples, are you?" He denied it and said, "I am not!" One of the servants of the high priest, a relative of him whose ear Peter cut off, said, "Did I not see you in the garden with Him?" Peter then denied again, and immediately a rooster crowed.

Peter, the great champion of the faith, the man who was so bold and so closely identified with the Savior, denied his Lord. He was devastated, but he couldn't take it back. Doubting Thomas and Denying Peter each made one little mistake, but their mistakes cost both of them their reputation.

Is it possible that you're about to make an inglorious mistake? Are you about to do something that you'll regret forever? Will one little foolish act take your precious name and demolish your reputation permanently? Don't do it. Ask God to give you strength and keep you from sin. Determine that by the power of the Holy Spirit you will not allow one slipup to destroy your life. You don't have to be remembered as a doubter, a denier, an adulterer or anything equally infamous. Remember this pearl of wisdom: "A good name is better than precious ointment."

Ending Well

Contrast those in the Bible who are remembered for one slipup with those who are remembered for ending well. One man comes to mind immediately as someone who finished as well as he began—Joseph.

He had walked with the Lord all his life. Even when others doubted him, he never doubted himself (Gen. 37). Even when others tempted him, he never succumbed to that temptation (Gen. 39). In Genesis 50:24 Joseph said to his brothers, "I am dying; but God will surely visit you, and bring you out of this land to the land of which He swore to Abraham, to Isaac, and to Jacob." As Joseph began, Joseph ended. His good name was intact at the end because he remembered this pearl of wisdom: "A good name is better than precious ointment."

And what about Caleb? He understood this pearl of wisdom too. Caleb was an old man when he said, "Give me this mountain of which the LORD spoke in that day; for you heard in that day how the Anakim were there, and that the cities were great and fortified. It may be that the LORD will be with me, and I shall be able to drive them out as the LORD said" (Josh. 14:12). Furthermore, Caleb did exactly what he believed God would enable him to do. At age 85, he drove out the Anakim and claimed that territory for himself. He finished well. His good name was preserved.

Andrew Bonar, a great preacher of Glasgow, Scotland, during the last century, was reminded frequently of what his father used to say to him: "Andrew, pray that both of us may wear well to the end." What he meant was, "Don't go out with a bang. Go out with a good name."

Tips on preserving your reputation

We all agree on the importance of preserving our good name, but how do we do that? Begin by remembering that your character is a reflection of everything you are, and your good name is a reflection of your character.

Character is everything that makes you you—everything you are, everything you do in secret, everything you do in public, everything you think, everything you say. That's your character. When your character is good, your name is good. And when your name is good, it reflects on your character.

A.W. Tozer, a great preacher and powerful man of God, said that we're known by the following seven things:

1. By what we want most.
2. By what we think about most.
3. By how we use our money.
4. By what we do with our leisure time.
5. By the company we keep and the company we enjoy.
6. By who and what we admire.
7. By what we laugh at.

These things form our reputation, and then reflect the reputation we have formed. We must keep them in mind if indeed we are going to be used of the Lord and have a good name at the end of our lives.

Furthermore, you can maintain a good name if you remember that it is far more easily maintained than it is regained. It's better to protect your character than to try to get it back after you've tarnished it. Thomas Paine apparently understood Solomon's pearl of wisdom when he said, "Character is much better kept than recovered."

A few years ago some well-known TV evangelists fell into serious sin. It affected every pastor, every church, every mission agency. It affected radio ministries like Back to the Bible. Ministries that were absolutely pure and free from the careless habits of others were deemed guilty by association. The cause of Christ suffered immensely and innocent people were lumped in with the guilty. Later, when the American public was asked the four sleaziest ways to make a living, they listed them in this order: being a drug dealer, being an organized crime boss, being a television evangelist and being a prostitute.

It's a shame that a few people are able to tarnish the character of many, but it happens. Character and a good name are far more easily maintained than they are regained. Purposefully live in such a way that you protect your good character. Don't try to repair it after it's lost. Take the time to keep it strong now.

Finally, you can maintain your good character if you remember that it's established as much by what you're against as what you're for. This is not a popular message in this day of moral relativism. But good people need to stand up for good things, and they need to speak out against bad things.

An Irishman came to the United States years ago to look for work, but things hadn't gone so well for him. He was being tried for a petty offense in a Kansas town. When the judge asked him if there was anyone who could vouch for his character, the man replied, "Your Honor, there's the sheriff." Stunned, the sheriff said, "Your Honor, I don't even know this man." But the Irishman came back to the judge in a flash and said, "See, I've lived in this country for more than twelve years, and the sheriff doesn't know me. Isn't that a reflection on my character?"

Sometimes attesting to our character depends on who knows us and will vouch for us. Other times it depends on those who do not know us well because we have maintained our character so well.

Make sure your character is so stellar, so upright, so pleasing to the Lord that when you need a character reference, it's the pastor they call on, not the local sheriff. Your good name is a reflection of who you are. Make sure it's a right reflection.

One pearl of wisdom that will be important to you all the days of your life and especially at the end of your life is this: "A good name is better than precious ointment." Never give up your good name. A good name is to be chosen over great riches (Prov. 22:1). That's a pearl of wisdom that will keep you until your final breath.

CHAPTER NINE

Remembering God

Pearl of Wisdom

*"Remember now your Creator in the days
of your youth, before the difficult days come,
and the years draw near when you say,
'I have no pleasure in them.'"*
Ecclesiastes 12:1

When my son, Tim, was about 14 years of age, we were visiting my mother and father in western Pennsylvania. My father was outside on a ladder at the top floor of his house washing windows. Tim opened a window, stuck his head out and said, "Whatcha doin', old man?" If there's one thing you never did to my father, it was to call him "old man." He thought that was disrespectful. So what did my father do? He turned the hose on Tim. Today my son is a pastor, but he never forgot that lesson. It made a mark on his life that he still remembers.

That's what Solomon means with this pearl of wisdom, "Remember now your Creator." The Hebrew word translated "remember" is *zakar*, but it means more than just "to think about." The word also means "to mark so as to recognize or to recount at a later time." It's also a command to revere God and keep His commandments. Then when you're old, you can look back on those days and draw strength from them. When you're 60 or 70 or 80, you want to be able to look back to the days of 16 and 18 and recognize God's hand on your life.

Moses recorded these same thoughts in Deuteronomy 8:18-19: "And you shall remember [*zakar*] the LORD your God, for it is He who gives you power to get wealth, that He may establish His covenant which He swore to your fathers, as it is this day. Then it shall be, if by any means you forget the LORD your God, and follow other gods, and serve them and worship them, I testify against you this day that you shall surely perish." Take note of the correlation between remembering God and prospering, and between forgetting God and perishing.

Many young people today are perishing because they've chased after the gods of money, sex and popularity. They're dying of sexually transmitted diseases because they've bought into the world's lie about safe sex. There is such a thing as safe sex, but not as popular culture depicts it. God invented safe sex, and He did so when He ordained heterosexuality, monogamy and fidelity in marriage. Yet so many teenagers are perishing because they've forgotten what it means to honor God in their youth. The U.S. Children's Fund reports that every day six teenagers commit suicide in America. Every day 16,833 women get pregnant in America, and 2,740 of them are just teenagers. Of these teenagers, 1,105 will have abortions.

Admittedly, this is a tough time to be a teen. By embracing sexual immorality, values-free education and irresponsible or apathetic parenting, society has deluded many young people to the point that they don't know what is right and what is wrong—or even if there is a right and wrong. That's why they need to remember their Creator in the days of their youth, and that means to have a clear understanding of who God is and what He requires.

Psalm 119:55 says, "I remember Your name in the night, O LORD, and I keep Your law." That's the word *zakar* again. Notice the connection between remembering and keeping God's law. Remembrance is always linked to obedience. When Solomon says, "Remember now your Creator in the days of your youth," he's not talking about just thinking back on God; he's talking about obeying God.

In Ecclesiastes 11:9-10 Solomon exhorts, "Rejoice, O young man, in your youth, and let your heart cheer you in the days of your youth; walk in the ways of your heart, and in the sight of your eyes; but know that for all these God will bring you into judgment. Therefore remove sorrow from your heart, and put away evil from your flesh, for childhood and youth are vanity." This means that Ecclesiastes 12:1, our pearl of wisdom in this chapter, is written in the context of a young man or a young woman recognizing right from wrong and choosing to live rightly.

If young people are to "remember God," they've got to get a clue as to what is right and what is wrong. And the only way for them to know right from wrong is to get back to the Bible. They're certainly not going to learn that distinction from television, the Internet, their peers or the magazines they read. They're only going to learn it from God's Word. We have to help our young people learn that "to remember God in the days of their youth" means to respect, obey and serve God.

But having reverence for God is as much caught as it is taught. As you teach your teenagers to revere God, they must also see it in your life. They must see it in what you do on Sunday. They must see it in how you respond to God in times of crisis. They must see it in what you say to them and what you do when you think they're not looking. That's the way we teach reverence for God.

Furthermore, there's the lesson of obedience. The habits of obedience are best formed during the periods of our greatest potential rebellion. Think about that. When is the greatest rebellion in a person's life? Generally it's during adolescence. Being a teenager is tough. That's the time when we have the greatest potential for rebellion, but that's also the time when we need to develop the greatest habits of obedience.

Learning to serve

The same is true for service. It's encouraging to see that a lot of teenagers are getting on the bandwagon of some sort of service these days. The number of teenagers between the ages of 12 and 17 in America doing volunteer work has increased 7 percent since 1992. When you ask these teenagers why they are volunteering their time, 84 percent of them say they feel a compassion for the needy. The same number say the cause for which they are volunteering time is important to them. That's a healthy sign in our society. But there's more to service than just volunteering time in social work. Service for the Lord needs to be learned as a young teenager as well.

I remember clearly the youth group I attended at Park Gate Baptist Church when I was about 16. My father was pastor of the church. We had a small youth group of about 20 kids. It was 1960 and there was a teen convention in Winona Lake, Indiana, that the teens of my church wanted to attend. My father went to the elder board and said, "Look, if these teens earn their way, will the church promise to pay for all the teens to go to this convention?" The church agreed and set up a program. They decided that if the teens attended Sunday morning, Sunday night and Wednesday night service for six months plus got involved in the church, the congregation would pay their way. I suspect that some of the deacons assumed there wouldn't be anybody who could meet those criteria. You should have seen the look on those deacons' faces when 60 teenagers met all the requirements and the church had to put up the money for all those teens to go. Not only did each of us in the youth group meet the requirements, but the 40 or so friends we invited to the convention did too. That was the best money the church ever spent. Out of those 60 kids, 33 of them went on either to a Bible college, a Bible school or a Christian liberal arts college and prepared for some kind of full-time service for the Lord. Now that's an investment for eternity!

A time for mentoring

So what are you doing with your teenagers today? Are you criticizing them?

Are you running them down? Are you constantly against them? Or are you trying to mentor them? Are you trying to help them see what reverence to God and to others is all about? Are you letting them see you obey God and helping them form the habit of obedience during the period of their greatest potential for rebellion? Are you giving them the opportunity to learn service?

Young people need to "remember God" because He has a claim on their physical lives. It's no accident that Solomon called God our "Creator" in Ecclesiastes 12:1. The three greatest decisions anyone can make are usually decided by young people before they reach their mid-20s: the salvation of their souls, the choice of a life's work and the choice of a life's companion. If you're a young person making those decisions, you need to remember God has a claim on all that you are physically because He is your Creator.

But more than that, God has a claim on your spiritual life. He created you spiritually as well as physically. You were dead in your trespasses and sins, but He made you alive and He gave you a life worth living (Eph. 2:1-2). "For you were bought at a price; therefore glorify God in your body and in your spirit, which are God's" (1 Cor. 6:20). God had a plan for you spiritually long before the world began. Solomon urges you, "Remember now your Creator in the days of your youth," because God has a claim on your spiritual life. He is your Savior.

Difficult days ahead

But there's yet another reason why a

young person needs to remember his Creator, and that's because difficult days are ahead. Now I know that if you're 16 or 18 or 21, you think you've got the world by the tail on a downward swing. You think you're invincible. Nothing can keep you from success. But a different day is coming.

Some of you reading this aren't 16 or 18 or 21. Maybe you're over 60. If so, you're really in the second half of Ecclesiastes 12:1. The first half says, "Remember now your Creator in the days of your youth." The second half says, "before the difficult days come, when the years draw near when you say, 'I have no pleasure in them.'" The difference between youth and old age is this: When you're young, you run into trouble; when you're old, trouble runs into you. Solomon uses a play on words here. The word for "difficult" or "evil" days is exactly the same word used in the preceding verse, Ecclesiastes 11:10, where he says, "put away evil from your flesh."

If you don't put away evil from your flesh as a young person, difficult days will come as an older person. If you don't live righteously as a young person, you reap the fruit of unrighteousness as an older person. There are days of trouble ahead both for your body and for your mind. It's wise to serve the Lord in your youth because the days are coming when you will not be able to serve Him the way you once did.

Solomon describes those coming days as days of old age when physically we're not at the peak of our performance. In fact, look at verse 3: "In the day when the keepers of the

91

house tremble, and the strong men bow down; when the grinders cease because they are few, and those that look through the windows grow dim." He's talking about when your hands and your arms—the keepers of the house—shake involuntarily, and your legs, or strong men, become weak. When he talks about the grinders being few, he's talking about your teeth. The window growing dim is failing eyesight. And verse 4, "when the doors are shut in the streets, and the sound of grinding is low," refers to your failing ears. The bottom line is, learn early to revere, obey and serve the Lord, because the day is coming when you will look back on those years and think, *Why didn't I do more then because now I can't?*

I was saved as a child. I'm so glad that someone took the time to be interested in a five-year-old boy. Because I came to know the Lord at an early age, I was spared from a life filled with thrills and sorrows. Most people in their youth see only the thrills. But when they're older, often all they can look back on are the sorrows. God spared me from that, and in its place He put a lifetime of opportunity for service to Him. I wouldn't trade one sermon in a county jail, one visit to a nursing home, one opportunity to lead another teenager to the Lord, for all the thrills that would be destroying my life now. I wasn't the loser; I was the winner.

Any effort you make with children or teenagers is never a wasted effort. "Remember your Creator in the days of your youth." That's a pearl of wisdom worth remembering—whether you're a teenager trying to make your way through difficult years, or an older adult trying to steer a teen through those years.

CHAPTER TEN

The End of the Matter

Pearl of Wisdom
"Let us hear the conclusion of the whole matter: fear God and keep His commandments, for this is man's all."
Ecclesiastes 12:13

Sammy Davis Jr. died a victim of throat cancer in mid-May 1990. He was only 64. For years he drew the applause of packed houses as he sang and danced and cracked jokes. But he buried his pain in alcohol and cocaine, chasing the delusion that his "swinging" lifestyle somehow compensated for his two divorces, his estrangement from his children and his futile efforts to become what he thought others expected him to be. "I didn't like me," Davis told an interviewer in 1989, "so it made all the sense in the world to me that if you don't like yourself, you destroy yourself. My life was empty. I had drugs, booze and broads, and I had nothing."

Another famous man wrote these same thoughts several thousand years before Sammy Davis Jr. His name was Solomon. As Solomon wrote the Book of Ecclesiastes, he left no doubt what his theme was. He stated it both in the beginning of the book and the end. Ecclesiastes 1:2 says, "Vanity of vanities, all is vanity." When you get to the last chapter, he repeats this theme in verse 8: "Vanity of vanities, all is vanity."

The idea of vanity, of things being of no value, permeates this book. Unfortunately, these empty things tend to be what you and I major on in life. We spend all of our time, all of our talent, all of our money on these things, and the Bible says they come to nothing. As you read through Ecclesiastes, you see so many things that Solomon concluded were meaningless, things like toil (1:14), wisdom (2:15), our prestige (4:16), our pleasures (2:1-2), even our wealth (5:10). When the Preacher (Solomon himself) said, "All is vanity," he meant everything in life.

Labor is vain

A recent study done of 4,126 male business executives revealed widespread dissatisfaction with their corporate experience. Forty-eight percent of all middle managers said that despite years of striving to achieve their professional goals, their lives seemed empty and meaningless. Sixty-eight percent of senior executives said that they had neglected their family life in order to pursue their professional goals. Half of them said that they would spend less time working and more time with their wives and children if they could start all over again. And the question that a lot of busy executives are asking themselves today is, What am I doing all this for? What is the purpose of my life?

In Ecclesiastes 2:4, Solomon, the richest man in the world, confronted these same issues. He said:

I made my works great, I built myself houses, and planted myself vineyards. I made myself gardens and orchards, and I planted all kinds of fruit trees in them. I made myself waterpools from which to water the growing trees of the grove. I acquired male and female servants, and had servants born in my house. Yes, I had greater possessions of herds and flocks than all who were in Jerusalem before me. I also gathered for myself silver and gold and the special treasures of kings and of the provinces. I acquired male and female singers, the delights of the sons of men, and musical instruments of all kinds. So I became great and excelled more than all who were before me in Jerusalem. Also my wisdom remained with me. Whatever my eyes desired I did not keep from them. I did not withhold my heart from any pleasure, for my heart rejoiced in all my labor; and this was my reward from all my labor. Then [and here's the catch] I looked on all the works of my hands. Then I looked on all the works that my hands had done and on the labor in which I had toiled; and indeed all was vanity and grasping for the wind. There was no profit under the sun (Eccles. 2:6-11).

That's a real downer! Here's a man who had everything. He had big houses, huge waterpools and lots of male and female servants. This man had singers and musicians in his house, employed around the clock, just to make life perfect. And yet he looked at all of that and saw the immediate futility of all of his labor. In fact, in verse 18 he says, "Then I hated all my labor in which I had toiled under the sun because I must leave it to the man who will come after me."

The lesson we learn is that you can work hard all the days of your life. You can squirrel away everything you make. You can hide it away in bank accounts, put it under the mattress, do with it whatever you want. But the day will come when you look back on all of it and it will be vanity, and you'll leave it to the one who follows you.

That's not to say that we aren't suppose to labor or that labor isn't good for us. It's not to say that we aren't to work hard with our hands and do what God wants us to do. Labor is the gift of God. He gives us the ability to work. Labor is not wrong—unless, of course, we fail to see what our labor is designed to do. If we keep all the fruits of our labor for ourselves, when we come to the end of our lives we've lost it all. If you're not laboring for something beyond yourself, then your life is meaningless.

Love is vanity

In Ecclesiastes 9:1, Solomon says, "For I considered all this in my heart so that I could declare it all. And the righteous and the wise and their works are in the hand of God. People know neither love nor hatred by anything that is before them." Later, in verses 4-6 he says, "But for me who is joined to all the living, there is hope. For a living dog is better than a dead lion. For the living know that they will die, but the dead know nothing. And they have no more reward, for the memory of them is forgotten.

Also their love, their hatred, their envy have now perished. Nevermore will they have a share in anything done under the sun."

Finally, in verse 9 we read, "Live joyfully with the wife whom you love all the days of your vain life which He has given you under the sun, all your days of vanity, for that is your portion in life and in the labor which you perform under the sun."

Solomon has moved from the subject of labor to the subject of love. Some of you can identify with the futility of your loves. Very few people today belong to what we would call the traditional family. Historically the traditional family consisted of one husband married to one wife, whom he truly loved. He was entirely faithful to her. And there was one wife who loved her husband and was entirely faithful to him, and usually two or more children. Children learned what faithfulness and love were all about from the example of their parents. At least that's the way it used to be. That's not the way it is today. The family unit I've just described accounted for 60 percent of all American families back in 1960. Today, that kind of family unit describes only 3 percent of American households.

We can see a futility of love everywhere in the world. You can see it not only in the divorce rate, but in the significant number of adults who will enter their marriage assuming that it will end in divorce. Many godly Christian women are saying, "I know exactly what that's like." You wonder if there are any godly men out there. And even if the men you date are godly men, many of them have had sexual encounters before they were saved. Certainly the blood of Jesus Christ can cleanse us from all sin, but this is still hardly an ideal dating pool for women who have remained pure and chaste all their lives.

My heart goes out to you who have experienced the pain of infidelity. I'm concerned for young, godly men and women who have become gun-shy in love because of bad experiences. Our society is a good example of why the writer of Ecclesiastes speaks about the vanity and the vexation of love. There is a real pearl of wisdom here.

Life is vanity

Consider another area in which the writer of Ecclesiastes says there is futility. Ecclesiastes 6:11 says, "Since there are many things that increase vanity, how is man the better? For who knows what is good for man in life, all the days of his vain life which he passes like a shadow? Who can tell a man what will happen after him under the sun?" Life itself often seems futile and meaningless. We've seen the results of such futility, even in young people, in places like Pearl, Mississippi; Jonesboro, Arkansas; and Paducah, Kentucky.

Every passage I've mentioned so far from the Book of Ecclesiastes has been somewhat bleak. They seem to say, "What's the point of life? You're born, you grow, you die." Have you ever asked that? Maybe you have a teenage son who has asked that. It's this very sense of futility that plagues some teenagers today, and many of them are committing suicide as a result. Does the writer of Ecclesiastes come to any conclusions?

How does he believe we should attack the problem of this futility of our lives?

The missing ingredient

The writer's conclusion is simple. It represents one of the great pearls of wisdom in the Book of Ecclesiastes. While there is enjoyment in labor, the immediate futility of labor overwhelms it. We amass wealth, we work hard, and we leave it to someone else. And while there is enjoyment in love, the immediate futility of love overwhelms it. We love and we're frequently hurt by someone who says he or she loves us but really doesn't. Furthermore, while there's enjoyment in life, the immediate futility of life overwhelms it. Frequently things don't go as we had planned and everything is ruined. So what's the point? Well, my friend, if your labors and your loves and your life seem futile, maybe there's a missing ingredient. Ecclesiastes 12:13 says, "Fear God and keep His commandments, for this is the whole duty of man."

What the Bible offers you is hope. God sent His Son, Jesus Christ, to fill the voids of your labors, to fill the voids of your loves, to fill the voids of your life. When you labor for eternal reward, not just temporal gain, when you serve mankind because you love Jesus, when you do in your life the things that bring joy and fulfillment forever, and not just temporal fulfillment, then you find you're keeping the commandments of God and you're enjoying life a whole lot more.

What are you doing in your life? Have you paid any attention to the great pearls of wisdom from God in Ecclesiastes? If you have, you know that there's more to life than living for yourself. You know there's more to life than loving. You know there's more to life than laboring. There's eternity. If you've never trusted Jesus Christ as your Savior for all eternity, I offer you the opportunity of a lifetime—to receive new life, eternal life. The apostle John wrote, "For God so loved the world that He gave His only begotten Son, that whoever believes in Him should not perish but have everlasting life" (John 3:16). You can receive forgiveness from your sins and be on your way to Heaven. Just tell the Lord that you know you're a sinner. Ask Him to save you. And when you ask Him, He will. That's what gives hope to a life of vexation and vanity. And that, my friend, is what will give hope to you.

The greatest pearl of wisdom is the pearl that brings you to the end of yourself and from there to Jesus. If life seems futile to you, trust Jesus Christ as Savior and discover a life worth living.

CONCLUSION

We all know that a pearl is the product of pain. When a diver finds a pearl in an oyster, he knows that a tiny grain of sand found its way inside the oyster's shell and the oyster secreted a milky substance to coat the grain of sand and ease the irritation it caused. Thus, pearls are precious not only because they are rare, but also because they are the result of much agony.

Wisdom is that way as well. Most wisdom is the product of pain. We try. We make a mistake. We fail. We learn. If we learn from our mistakes, they have been valuable to us. If we do not, we are fools.

Much of the wisdom of God's Word is contained in the "wisdom literature" portion of the Bible, which is the Psalms, Proverbs, Ecclesiastes and the Song of Solomon. The Psalms are inspiring Hebrew poetry. The Proverbs are pithy, sententious sayings. The Song of Solomon is an ode to love. But the Book of Ecclesiastes is a corpus of wisdom related to a single theme— the vanity of man's life apart from God. That means the wisdom we glean from Ecclesiastes is practical wisdom, wisdom that keeps us from meaninglessness.

We all can attest to the fact that the ten pearls of wisdom featured in this book have accomplished their desired goal. Whether it's viewing life with an eye on God's timetable or viewing our wealth as His special gift to us, the pearls of wisdom from the

Book of Ecclesiastes, if practiced, will keep us from empty living. The key, of course, is that we must practice this wisdom, and the reason is the fitting conclusion to this book of wisdom: "For God will bring every work into judgment, including every secret thing, whether it is good or whether it is evil" (Eccles. 12:14).

Don't practice the wisdom of God to get better at it. Practice it because without it, life is robbed of its meaning. Treasure these ten pearls. Read them again and again. Practice them. Pass them on to someone important to you. After all, they are God's pearls. That makes them priceless.